KU-731-104

Defending Europe in the 1990s

WITHDRAWN

Studies in International Political Economy will present new work, from a multinational stable of authors, on major issues, theoretical and practical, in the international political economy.

General Editor

Susan Strange, Professor of International Relations, London School of Economics and Political Science, England

Consulting Editors

Ladd Hollist, Visiting Associate Professor, Brigham Young University, USA

Karl Kaiser, Director, Research Institute of the German Society for Foreign Affairs, Bonn, and Professor of Political Science, University of Cologne, West Germany

William Leohr, Graduate School of International Studies, University of Denver, USA

Joseph Nye, Professor of Government, Harvard University, USA

Already Published

The Political Economy of New and Old Industrial Countries
The East European Economies in the 1970s
Defence, Technology and International Integration
Japan and Western Europe
Tax Havens and Offshore Finance
The North–South Dialogue
The International Gold Standard
Transnational Oil

Forthcoming Titles

Dependency Transformed

Defending Europe in the 1990s

The New Divide of High Technology

Joseph C. Rallo

62461

OXFORD. OX1 2RL

 Frances Pinter (Publishers), London

© Joseph C. Rallo, 1986

First Published in Great Britain in 1986 by
Frances Pinter (Publishers) Limited
25 Floral Street, London WC2E 9DS

British Library Cataloguing in Publication Data
Rallo, Joseph C.
    Defending Europe in the 1990s
    1. Security, International   2. European Economic
    Community countries—Strategic aspects
    3. European Economic Community countries—Foreign
    relations
    I. Title
    327.1'16   D1058
    ISBN 0-86187-615-6

Typeset by Joshua Associates Limited, Oxford
Printed by SRP Ltd., Exeter

To my wife Michele and my father John for their support and inspiration and to my daughter Heather in the hope that her world may have less divisive issues than this to deal with.

Contents

Preface   xi

Introduction   xv

1. The division of sovereignty   1
2. Intra-Alliance sources of tension   10
3. The legacy of Community failures in high technology   45
4. Structural obstacles to new Community responses   64
5. The coalescing of a European security policy   81
6. A new European security policy: the choice of institution   109
7. Prospects   128
Index   131

List of Tables

1. Department of Defense—B/A by appropriation 16
2. Federal budget trends 30
3. Anglo-American and German–American relations 35
4. Public opinion on NATO and Europe's security-policy role 38
5. Sympathy for European peace demonstrations 39
6. Sympathy for a move towards neutralism in East–West conflict 40
7. Share by region of computer hardware market held by firms 52
8. World market in electric and electronic materials: Europe's deteriorating position 57
9. Aircraft markets by region 58
10. National government aid to the European aerospace industry 59
11. Commission and industrial projections for aircraft, 1975–85 61
12. Trade balances for high-technology goods, 1970 and 1982 65
13. NATO country defence spending 115
14. Burden-sharing 116
15. Comparison of defence burdens 116

List of Figures

1. Fiscal 1985 science and technology programme 28
2. A proposed European technology policy (ETP) structure 104

Acknowledgement

Research funded by a 1984–5 Grant for Research into European Integration from the Commission of the European Communities.

The opinions of this work are those of the author alone and do not represent the views of the European Communities, the United States Air Force Academy or the United States Department of Defense.

The exchange rate used throughout this book is based on the following figures: £1 = $1.38 and £1 = 0.75 ECU.

Preface

The ideal of a united Europe remains a compelling and powerful vision. A regional union comprising human, technological, economic and military resources on a par with either superpower has tantalized since the demise of the pre-World War Two system of ordering international relations. Nurtured by a global system predicated on American leadership, Europe was free to fashion a new method of defining its relations. Adrift within the global environment, Europeans anchored their political and security futures to the United States and focused their attention on economic matters within the Common Market. Unique in its quasi-sovereign attributes, the Market became an independent vehicle further to align and integrate the entire spectrum of European relations.

Early and somewhat naïve views of what was attainable soon floundered on national identities, values and objectives. Inability to bring security issues within the Community's mandate reflected the post-war division in European sovereignty which included continued dependence on the United States for military protection and a secondary status in the international economic environment. Gradually, though, the American economic role came to be viewed in competitive terms as its multinationals assumed control and direction of key industrial sectors integral to the development of Europe. Nominal adherence to the vision of a united Europe evaporated as members scrambled to tighten national control of economic levers in an attempt to reassume primacy over policy direction. Ineffectual national responses coexisted uneasily with regional plans, both unable to stem the loss of control or to re-establish equity in responsibility at international levels. Integration, derailed into petty squabbles, became a by-product of national policies rather than the central focus of internally generated initiatives and objectives.

Europe now stands, as so often before, at a crossroads. Economic cooperation has proved successful but often only on an *ad hoc* basis separate from the political undertones that give those relationships direction. Technological capability exists but is so fragmented as to tempt with a vision often impossible to achieve. Military output and preparation for defence depend either on export to the Third World or on NATO arrangements. National priorities and regional objectives compatible on paper appear unbridgeable in practice. The vision of Europe remains but the manner and means of its achievement are lost in studies.

This volume seeks to provide direction to the vision of union by distilling the very real issues now facing Europe into two challenges. The first is the changing international environment, no longer grounded on American dominance, which provides the opportunity for the re-emergence of Europe as a major global actor. The impetus for European cooperative action is now no longer internally derived but must exist instead as a counter to a global environment increasingly antithetical to such action. Not to act is to acquiesce in a global realignment with no special incentive to advance European interests. The second challenge is to choose the manner of response. Here we find a rare area of agreement which acknowledges that action must be in those industrial areas capable of sustaining and enhancing a long-term European global presence. The domain of high technology therefore provides the instrument of a European response to both challenges.

This choice of instrument and of objective, then, allows the three legacies of an antiquated European state system to be remedied. The dictates of high technology require coordination of resources. Fragmented national systems are increasingly incapable of unilaterally addressing global challenges. Coordination, whether by a strict division of labour or more gently through aggregation and central direction of resources, mandates a more open regional system of shared information, personnel and resources. Regional direction of high technology capabilities though must be combined with national control over traditional economic spheres to insure policy coherence as well as public support of program implementation.

The second concern for regional action is more political than economic and seeks coherence through policy cohesion. An economically integrated Europe is incapable of assuming a position as superpower without a greater sense of political compatibility. While not implying the objective of a single European government there is the need to end the artificial separation of defence and economic issues now pursued within NATO and the European Community. To assume a major American role in the former is to negate cooperative efforts in the latter. A merger of European responsibility under the rubric of security policy must ensue. The instrument of high technology provides that opportunity, given the 'dual use' of most of its outputs. European commercial cooperation in pursuit of global consumer markets carries with it the opportunity to plan simultaneously not just military strategy but also the weaponry essential to its implementation.

The final fragment is the need to make this sense of a coherent Europe relevant to the public. While passports and currency are visible symbols it is the need to address the more basic issue of quality of life that is fundamental. Security planning when responsive to one's own elected officials is far more palatable and thus more coherently pursued than when that posture is deemed a response to a dominant alliance partner no matter how well respected.

Introduction

This is a study on the feasibility of establishing a security relationship in the European Community (EC) to enhance its member roles within the transatlantic NATO alliance. This is not a treatise on weapons, doctrine, or defence policy, although these topics are intrinsic to the debate. In a similar fashion this is not a theoretical study of global power politics decrying the secondary position of Europe in that struggle. It is, rather, an effort to suggest what a unique regional entity, the Community, whose members are for the most part developed Western democracies, might do to achieve a security role commensurate with its economic resources and consistent with its political objectives. From this perspective security policy manages political, economic, social as well as military resources and issues in a formula meshing national and regional institutions, objectives and, above all, will. The study is not a blueprint for action but a treatment of issues, programmes and policies centering on the theme of European cooperation in pursuit of stature and influence in an increasingly competitive global security environment.

While there will be little attempt to suggest a theory capable of defining and prescribing this process, it would be remiss to suggest that this activity is bereft of any rationale, occurring in a haphazard fashion as a response to short-term events and personalities. Indeed one of the obstacles to any treatment of Community activities is the welter of theory, prescription and formula that have accompanied the process of a coalescing Europe. The following sections briefly discuss and discard traditional theories of regional integration before suggesting a framework which allows Community aspirations and goals for the issue of security policy to be most persuasively articulated.

Three issues in particular distinguish this proposed framework from previous efforts:

1. European union as a distinct objective is inconsistent with member attitudes and should be shelved;
2. harmonization of member objectives, acknowledging the primacy of

intergovernmental bargaining, accepting the probability of a 'two-speed' Europe and limiting the requisite of centralization, should be officially accepted and adopted as policy guidance;
3. the outdated bargain of the Common Agricultural Policy (CAP) should be replaced by an equivalent commitment to a high-technology industrial policy with its dual implications for defence and civilian applications.

In sum, theory must acknowledge that while Community relations seek internal coherence and compatibility, there is a simultaneous need to accommodate this process to the increased internationalization of issues facing member and region alike. To focus on integration is to assume an insularity of the region, an outcome at odds with the desired international role envisaged by Europe, especially with respect to its evolving security policy.

THE CONCEPT OF REGIONAL INTEGRATION: BASIC THEORIES

The literature concerning regional integration is vast, often contradictory and generally reflective of the underlying lack of consensus on the permanent implications of intraregional cooperation. For the purpose of this study the following definition of integration as a development process will be utilized: 'A process whereby a group of people organized initially in two or more independent nation-states, come to constitute a political whole which in some sense can be described as a community'.[1] Two themes are implicit in this definition. First, that any learning process must affect all levels of the states participating in the integration plan. Thus political socialization of the individual as well as institutional restructuring of the state are central concepts in the reorganization process. Second, that at some point this process of community building requires a shift in institutional responsibility from the national to the regional level. The manner in which the region is allowed to exercise this responsibility is neither preordained nor pre-emptive of continued parallel national activity in individual planning sectors.

   The four basic theories of integration may, therefore, be assessed by tracing their presentation of the twin themes of political socialization and institutional development in pursuit of national restructuring consistent with an evolving regional security policy. Basic to each theory is the idea that existing national systems are unable to cope with the demands made on their resources. Some form of regional harmonization is therefore implicit in each of the four approaches.

Functionalism

Functionalism suggests that the state's ability successfully to deliver essential social and economic services will be increased by pooling and dispensing the resources of several nations according to a more effective regional system. This new regional institutional system would initially require national cooperation in socio-economic activities, leaving the 'high' politics of foreign and security affairs to the exclusive control of state officials. Functionalists, such as David Mitrany, suggested that a self-sustaining cycle of regional cooperation would result from this new institutional structure.[2] Improved delivery of services would lend support to the organization providing those services. Both institutional officials and individual recipients of those services would become increasingly socialized to the idea of cooperation and would then demand the expansion of this system to other areas of regional activity. This concept of 'spill-over' suggested that regional integration would then follow a single course from technical cooperation in the delivery of selected services through economic union until the objective of a comprehensive political/security community was achieved.[3] The establishment of the European Coal and Steel Community (ECSC) in 1952 was seen as the first step in that direction for the members of the Community.

Functionalism as a planning concept for integration has proved ineffective essentially because its division between socio-economic and political activities is not shared by national officials. The continuing conflict in Italy between the industrial North and the agricultural South illustrates the reality that delivery of services is made on essentially political grounds.[4] Even when such a distinction is possible it generally results from the acknowledged inability of the new institution to spill over into other areas of regional activity. This is essentially what happened to the ECSC and to Euratom, whose areas of control remain what they were when the former was established in 1952 and the latter in 1958.[5] Altiero Spinelli articulated this concern when he stated that the separation of the political from the socio-economic sphere actually lessened the integrating potential of a region which, by definition, required a primarily political solution.[6] Finally, while functional institutions might establish programmes, their implementation within the Community is by way of existing national systems. Practice has shown that national programmes often do not give the credit due to the role played by regional institutions and resources.[7] As a result the socializing potential of such cooperative activity fails to materialize, let alone serve as the basis for more comprehensive regional activity. Functional cooperation as the basis for security integration has therefore failed because of an inability to expand beyond its original narrowly defined mandate of responsibility.

Pluralism

Pluralism seeks to develop intergovernmental communication patterns which go beyond mere conflict resolution and instead establish a permanent system for cooperative regional planning. Unlike the functionalist emphasis on regional institutional structures, pluralists view integration in terms of the levels of interaction existing between participating national systems. A successful pluralist system, even though lacking shared institutions of government, is still identified by a high degree of communication and responsiveness to mutually articulated national objectives. Karl Deutsch first suggested that the degree of integration within pluralist regions might be measured in terms of the shared culture and level of interaction existing within the system.[8] Deutsch assumed that nations maintaining high levels of such contacts were more integrated than those exhibiting lesser levels, notwithstanding the presence of formal regional ties in either case. Transaction flows measured by trade, tourist and mail contacts were used to determine the rate of such interaction between the national units and citizens of a particular area. High levels of interaction were said to represent the process of socialization in support of a further increase in the nature and extent of such contacts. A successful process of socialization would lead to either a 'pluralistic' or an 'amalgamated' security community depending on the institutional structure adopted for the area.[9]

Pluralism, as presented by Deutsch and others, failed to provide a clear conceptual framework to explain the process of regional integration. Methodologically, Deutsch's use of the Relative Acceptance (RA) Index to measure transaction flows has been severely criticized, leaving his theoretical framework without empirical support.[10] Even if the RA Index data were to be accepted it is difficult to understand how transactions at the individual level would accelerate the process of integration which requires agreement and commitment at the elite levels. But pluralism as a theory essentially fails because of its inability to present policy-makers with a realistic framework within which to structure regional programmes. By concentrating on factors of socialization to the complete exclusion of institutional structures, pluralism limits the ability of planners to fashion new systems to channel the learning process gradually in favour of regional solutions. This absence of structure to guide the process of national accommodation to regional objectives is fatal to the utilization of pluralism as a planning concept for security harmonization.

Federalism

Federalism encompasses the familiar position that a new regional institutional system may be established by adopting a constitutional framework which transfers power to a central authority, thus creating a federal structure in place of previously separate national units.[11] This process of nation-building may be viewed as a continuum of choices running from a unitary state like the Netherlands through federalism to a confederal union such as Canada.[12] Federalism might be an attractive planning option within a particular state, but its applicability to a region consisting of established national units is less certain. The Canadian experience of trying to establish a federal unit within one national system is suggestive of the problems that might arise if a similar effort were to be seriously pursued within the Community.

In fact the desire directly to impose a federal structure within the Community, loosely viewed as a United States of Europe, has rarely been heard outside the camp of followers of Jean Monnet.[13] Instead, Commission officials such as Spinelli have sought indirect ways to substitute a federal system in place of the present Community structure. Spinelli argued that national units were incapable of voluntarily dissolving themselves in order to create the supranational institutions that federalism requires.[14] Thus he suggested that a federal system might be indirectly imposed by means of a popularly elected European Parliament with the capability to require the gradual transfer of national political competence to regional supranational institutions. The popular election of the European Parliament in 1979 was viewed as the first step in Spinelli's vision of a federal system for the Community.

Notwithstanding its popular election the limited institutional role allowed the Parliament clearly reflects the lack of support for a federal structure on the part of the Community's members. The continuous transfer of policy-making control from the Commission and the Council of Ministers to the European Council clearly indicates the desire on the part of members to retain ultimate planning responsibility in their hands. It has also been suggested that the direct election of members to Parliament isolates them from national policy-making structures and further limits their ability to articulate European concerns at home.[15]

Federalism, because of its clarity and comprehensiveness, remains a powerful symbol periodically raised to renew member commitment to the objectives of a united Europe. The 1972 Paris Summit declaration of 'political community by 1980' was such an effort.[16] More recently the 1981 Genscher–Colombo formula and the current Franco-German resolution for a new treaty consistent with federal objectives have reassumed the path worn by those earlier initiatives.[17] Whether they will be successful will be more a matter of national will than support for a theory whose place in rearranging established inter-state relations is still uncertain.

Neo-functionalism

Successfully combining the twin themes of political socialization and institutional development, neo-functionalism ultimately emerged as the principal theory associated with regional integration. Integration for the neo-functionalist results from the inability of existing national institutions to meet increased demands from limited economic resources. Unlike the gradual approach of the functionalists, this national shortfall provides the basis for immediately turning to regional institutions for assistance. Neo-functionalism emphasizes that this shifting of individual loyalties to regional supranational institutions is sustained by exploiting the inability of the nation to resolve adequately the issue of resource allocation on its own.[18] The theory is especially conducive to directing activities in the resource-constrained security-policy area.

Neo-functionalists generally focus their attention on the specific system that is to be created to resolve intraregional conflict.[19] Their concern with emerging institutions and policies for the region have made their views acceptable to Community planners who increasingly must shape theory to continuing patterns of national control. Neo-functionalism meshes easily with daily practice since the theory allows for growth as well as for disintegration in regional cooperation.[20] This flexibility has resulted in neo-functionalists viewing the process of integration as a series of cooperative actions within specific issue sectors rather than as part of a single developmental scheme. For neo-functionalists such as Ernst Haas, the progress of regional integration is to be measured by the amount of responsibility actually transferred to central institutions.[21] While this approach clearly reflects the actual practice of Community planning it does leave open the question of what the final institutional form of the Community will actually be.

Neo-functionalism, and indeed the general concept of integration theory, has been severely criticized by adherents of the traditional realist approach to international relations.[22] Stanley Hoffmann has presented the two arguments generally associated with this more traditional approach to international relations theory: first, that the process of Community formation is simply another example of traditional domestic policy-making instead of a wholly new approach to cooperative decision-making; second, that national preoccupation with regional objectives is only one of the issues of importance to the state and not the overriding one at that—especially when security concerns are engaged, the role and importance of the state remains paramount. Hoffmann concludes that any analysis must instead address individual state relations with the region and with the global system as two separate but closely related issues.[23]

Haas met these criticisms essentially by acknowledging their validity and then incorporating them in his later work. By dividing regional activity into separate issue sectors Haas acknowledges that national activity in one area does not necessarily result in a greater degree of cooperation at the regional level. In this manner there might be very little connection between cooperative planning in older policy sectors like the CAP and newer initiatives such as industrial policy. While intraregional concerns are central to the former area, resolution of the latter issue is contingent on cooperation with extraregional partners and organizations.[24] As a result the responsibility for these new issues will be shared by the nation and the region in a formula whose exact dimensions will be as varied as the problems, not the least of which is the demise of a central institutional structure with comprehensive regional policy-making responsibility. National planners will seek the best solution in a result that does not automatically favour a regional policy for the problem.[25] In this fashion Haas laid the groundwork to suggest that future policy initiatives might better be viewed in terms other than those associated with traditional theories of integration.

INTEGRATION AND INTERDEPENDENCE: TWO COMPETING THEORIES

This study will suggest that the Community's emerging security policy is more accurately analysed in interdependent than in integrative terms. Any restructuring of the international system requires compensatory changes in the relations between states comprising that system. Since the Community's security policy is a response to those changes, the intraregional relations of its members must similarly be affected by a realignment in that external system. The position of the Community as the world's largest trading system makes the region particularly sensitive to any changes affecting the terms of economic and industrial activity. Neither the internal dynamics created by the progress of integration nor the explicit policies of Community institutions have proved capable of preventing this realignment. Instead, national policies have been altered to reflect the need to include extraregional actors and institutions in any new planning proposals. In this manner interdependence, rather than integration, has come to be the concept that best summarizes national and regional activity within the Community ambit.

The formulation of interdependence theory, like that of integration, was an attempt to define relations between states in terms other than those of the realists. Interdependence is generally referred to as a condition of the relations existing between states and does not have the causal connotations of the term 'process' as utilized by integrationists. Oran Young describes interdependence as 'the extent to which events occurring in any given part or within any given component unit of a world system affect . . . events taking place in each of the other parts or component units of the system'.[26]

In much the same way as with integration theory, such relations may occur in different issue areas and may reach differing levels of intensity between the units involved.[27] But interdependence differs from integration theory in two important aspects. First is the overt political component present only in regional integration. Often referred to as the creation of a 'political community', this is the terminal point that the process of integration is expected to achieve:

Policy integration can be regarded as an attempt to reduce adverse costs of policy interdependence by deliberately coordinating policy and thus changing the nature of policy interdependence without necessarily reducing its level.[28]

The exact nature of this change is the acceptance of a unified policy administered by a central organization which combines both political and economic competency over the issue sector in question. This combination is possible only within the ambit of regional integration. Thus, while a single policy may exist in either an integrative or an interdependent setting, only a relationship that emphasizes this political component may properly be termed integration.

Second is the recognition within interdependence theory that asymmetric as well as symmetric relations may exist between states and between states and the international system as a whole. While this relationship is particularly explored in the North–South *dependencia* literature such asymmetries are not exclusive to that area.[29] One may suggest that the minimal dependence of OPEC members on the international economic system contributed to their ability to alter favourably their position within that external environment. Although integration theory recognizes the possibility of such an imbalance in progress, this is not specifically seen as the result of individual member dependence on the external system but is rather viewed as the product of intraregional discord. For Europe these asymmetries give rise to the option for different modes and manners of development even within the region, a process often termed a 'two-speed' Community.[30]

Paul Taylor, in his recent review of integration theory, reaches a similar conclusion. He suggests that three tendencies became apparent in the Community by the early 1980s, fixation on which negated progress on more practical policy options. These tendencies—a fear of centralization, expansion of membership, and an increased internationalization of issues—coalesced to sidetrack the search for policy direction because of the immediate need to seek short-term responses.[31] He concludes that a commonality of objectives rather than a concern with unification *per se* is the path best suited to accommodating these tendencies in the future.[32]

COMPLEX INTERDEPENDENCE AND SECURITY POLICY

To assert merely that interdependence theory characterizes Community realtions in a more plausible formula than does integration theory is to leave unanswered what shape those relations might assume in the future. Theory, although imperfect, should attempt to formulate guidelines to allow analysis of actual policy deviations from anticipated patterns. Any formulation that addresses the complexity of security policy must be capable of including the national, regional as well as international relations of the states involved. The formulation by Keohane and Nye under the title of 'complex interdependence' provides the theoretic and predictive construct best suited to an analysis of the emerging security policy in the European Community.[33]

Complex interdependence seeks to provide a comprehensive theory of international relations that avoids the dominance of military issues in traditional realism and the complete negation of the utility of force held by the modernists. Although Keohane and Nye accept both Young's and Deutsch's formulations of interdependence, they would term such reciprocity 'simple interconnectedness' unless there were costs associated with the contacts. Thus an equal trade balance between two states would yield different outcomes if one state dealt in perfume and the other in oil. One is more dependent on that continued relationship and would suffer greater costs were it to be terminated. Thus an essential component of complex interdependence are the asymmetries present in any relationship manipulation of which creates the potential for influence: 'when we say asymmetrical interdependence can be a source of power we are thinking of power as control over resources or the *potential* to affect outcomes'.[34]

The ability to influence a relationship is further separated into two dimensions, sensitivity and vulnerability: 'sensitivity means liability to costly effects imposed from outside before policies are altered to try to change the situation. Vulnerability can be defined as an actor's liability to suffer costs imposed by external events even after policies have been altered'.[35] Sensitivity and vulnerability dependence are both essential to the emerging security policy options for Europe. A continuation of present security relations as defined by the asymmetry in the NATO 'two-way street' favouring the United States is an example of sensitivity dependence. A change in relations through a restructuring of NATO or the development of an alternative European security structure would change the equation to one of vulnerability dependence. How costly are those adjustments to Europeans in terms of defence guarantees, export markets and employment patterns? Does the cost of creating a substitute to present security arrangements outweigh the gain in potential to effect outcomes more commensurate with European objectives? In their formulation vulnerability dependence is clearly more important in terms of providing power assets to actors and includes the security component that is minimized in sensitivity dependence.[36]

The final aspect of complex interdependence concerns the use of asymmetric dependence to effect outcomes. Power has been defined as a measure of influence over outcomes rather than the simple possession of resources.[37] Since the commitment of a more vulnerable actor to a particular issue might outweigh the resources of others in the relationship it is essential to understand the political bargaining process that occurs within the interdependent setting in order to explain outcomes.

COMPLEX INTERDEPENDENCE AND THE EUROPEAN COMMUNITY

Complex interdependence, then, seeks to address political and economic relations in an environment where power, in military terms, is not an acceptable instrument of persuasion. An environment is defined by the interactions that set particular states apart from the remainder of the global community. Since environments overlap they must be identified with reference to established rules governing specific relationships. Governing arrangements that affect relationships of interdependence are termed 'international regimes' by Keohane and Nye.[38] Such regimes serve to mediate between the global environment and those states privy to a regime. The nature of the regime determines its potential to affect outcomes on behalf of its members. Single-issue regimes such as OPEC may have a high intensity of influence in a narrow area, as compared to the broader scope but lower potential of NATO.

The European Community is recognized as an international regime unique in its potential to affect outcomes both within and external to the group. That institutional potential to affect external outcomes is dependent on the internal source of authority derived from member positions. In some sectors such as agriculture and trade, the Community has the power to define, implement and enforce agreements. Other sectors, such as industrial policy, are a mixture of Community and member inputs in a complex, often arcane, formula. Few areas, with the exception of strictly military issues, remain the sole province of member governments. Allocation of influence, both as to role and scope, remains an active process, with apparently settled topics often prodded into renewed controversy by events. This fluidity of bargaining thus particularly suits complex interdependence to the analysis of emerging Community initiatives in the area of security policy.

Keohane and Nye suggest that when complex interdependence is suited to anlaysis of an international regime three characteristics will be present which ensure that these relations will be demonstrably different than under conditions of realism or modernism. Those characteristics and their application to an analysis of European security policy will be briefly explored in the following sections.

Multiple channels of communication

The essence of complex interdependence is that states no longer act as single entities pursuing their national interests. In this fashion groups of actors pursuing their perceived interests combine to define governmental, national or regional positions and objectives. The multiplicity of actors in the area of security policy ensures a complex matrix of interests, issues and alliances compounded by the overlay of European goals on nationally or internationally directed actions. Compromise to manage these interactions is often more important than outcomes when anticipating positions and trade-offs in issue negotiations. The multiplicity of issues and actors intrinsic to the current European security debate and addressed by this study may be suggested by the following partial list:

regional: Esprit, Eureka
inter-governmental: WEU, EC, EPC, NATO
inter-state: Tornado and Airbus
domestic: pro-peace, anti-nuclear movements and parties
private industrial: multinational enterprises, defence contracts and commercial use of derived applications.

Absence of a hierarchy of issues

The negation of the utility of military force within a regime covered by complex interdependence requires that the policy agenda be defined by domestic and international pressures rather than mandated by the military threat endemic in an anarchic global environment. The agenda is therefore dominated by the 'low' issues of economics recognizing the political and policy implications that flow from their discussion or resolution. Differing perceptions of the need for national, regional or intergovernmental solutions are complicated by the resources and objectives that bound and define individual actors. Issue resolution is often less troublesome than agreement on what should constitute the agenda of regional activity. The sensitivity of security policy within Europe uniquely reflects this tension and translates into a multiplicity of avenues for resolution, each vying with the others for primacy given the absence of a prearranged issue hierarchy.

A sense of the difficulty present in resolving the issue of security in the absence of agreement on agenda or on overall policy direction will be developed in subsequent chapters. The inability to address directly the security topic is suggested by current efforts to engage the Community in the discussion by encompassing the matter within the rubric of industrial policy. The European response to the American Strategic Defense Initiative (SDI), currently subsumed within the proposed Eureka project, nicely illustrates the need to finesse a coordinated policy through competing interests and entrenched actors. Thus the European Parliament avidly discusses security policy while the Commission is unable even openly to admit that the topic is clearly within the Community's ambit.[39] Private pressure groups differ on the regional agenda depending on whether they would benefit or whether inclusion would divert resources and attention from their cause. Thus high-technology firms and CAP orientated producers differ markedly in perspective and willingness to include or exclude security policy on the regional agenda.

Transnational and transgovernmental relations

The absence of hierarchy among issues and multiple channels of communication combine effectively to diminish the ability of a government single-mindedly to pursue policy objectives. Programme implementation for issues such as security becomes as dependent on the management of transnational and transgovernmental relations as on traditional domestic processes. The enlargement of the scope of regional activities diminishes the ability to compartmentalize topics and increases the need to link issues. Linkage serves to extract concessions for one's own interests, however defined. Linkage within the Community's voting structure allows weak members to extract concessions on security related issues even though their direct role in that policy debate is minimal. Spain was able to ensure its Community accession in 1986 on favourable terms by linking membership to a positive vote on staying in NATO.[40] In turn, Greek reluctance to Spanish accession was deflected by the promise of several billion dollars in aid from Community and member resources.[41]

Issue linkage on security policy between major Community members tends to be more focused. West Germany's attempt to gain a more favourable role in the proposed Eureka project is furthered by simultaneously pursuing government and private links as subcontractor to American firms within the SDI. French efforts to enhance its role in Eureka are similarly being pursued by threatening to go its own way if other Europeans are not forthcoming in meeting their demands. Europe as a whole seeks a greater NATO role by suggesting the imminent conclusion of closer cooperation on issues such as procurement which would work to the detriment of American firms.

As these contacts proliferate, the opportunity to pursue several lines of policy options increases. At some point a statement of direction must emerge but given the multiplicity of actors at national and regional levels that time is not necessarily near. Thus the final and essential element of complex interdependence is the role of international organizations in the management of both the emerging and emergent policy stances of members on security policy.

THE ROLE OF INTERNATIONAL ORGANIZATIONS: THE EUROPEAN COMMUNITY AND EUROPEAN SECURITY POLICY

The book concludes with an examination of the reasons, proposals and probable outcomes underlying current efforts to develop a security policy for Europe. Of particular concern is the institutional form best suited to such an effort. The military, political, economic and social aspects of such a policy requires an institution capable of managing diverse and at times competing relationships and positions. It is generally acknowledged that one of the two organizations, the European Community or NATO, is best suited to expand its current mandate to assume responsibility for the entire spectrum of security-related issues and concerns. Ernst Haas has noted that military alliances, even with permanent organs and broad competence, historically have triggered little or no permanent interaction between members.[42] He then

suggests that only an entity such as the Community has that potential.[43] Haas's conclusion, then, becomes a favourable point of departure
for this study.

NOTES

1. Charles Pentland, *International Theory and European Integration* (New York: Free Press, 1973). p. 21.
2. David Mitrany, *A Working Peace System* (Chicago: Quadrangle Books, 1966).
3. Joseph Nye, *Peace in Parts* (Boston: Little, Brown and Company, 1971).
4. P. A. Allum, *Italy—Republic without Government* (New York: W.W. Norton and Company, 1973), pp. 20–32.
5. Eric Stein, Peter Hay and Michel Waelbroeck, *Documents for European Community Law and Institutions in Perspective* (New York: The Bobbs Merrill Company, Inc., 1976), pp. 1–40.
6. Altiero Spinelli, *The Eurocrats: Conflict and Crisis in the European Community* (Baltimore: Johns Hopkins University Press, 1966).
7. *Wall Street Journal*, 10 January 1975, p. 1.
8. Karl Deutsch, *Political Community and the North Atlantic Area* (Princeton: Princeton University Press, 1957).
9. Ibid., p. 17.
10. William Fisher, 'Analysis of the Deutsch Sociocausal Paradigm of Political Integration', *International Organization*, 23 (Winter 1969), pp. 254–90; Barry Hughes and John Schwartz, 'Dimensions of Political Integration and the Experience of the European Community', *International Organization*, 26 (September 1972), pp. 263–94.
11. Peter Hay, *Federalism and Supranational Organization* (Urbana: University of Illinois Press, 1966).
12. Joseph Nye, 'Comparative Regional Integration: Concept and Measurement', *International Organization*, 22 (Spring 1968), pp. 855–80.
13. Jean Monnet, 'A Ferment of Change' in Lawrence B. Krause, ed., *The Common Market: Progress and Controversy* (Englewood Cliffs, N.J.: Prentice-Hall, 1968), pp. 40–50.
14. Spinelli, op. cit.
15. Assembly of Western European Union, *WEU, European Union and the Atlantic Alliance*, 30th ordinary session, Doc. 990, 30 October 1984, p. 16.
16. *EC Bulletin*, October 1972, pp. 9–26.
17. 'Draft European Act', *EC Bulletin*, November 1981, pp. 87–91; 'Bid to Create a new European Dimension to Atlantic Pact', *The German Tribune*, 4 November 1983, p. 1; 'European Disunion', *The Economist*, 24 August 1985, pp. 12–13.
18. Ernst Haas, 'The Study of Regional Integration—Reflections on the Joy and Anguish of Pre-theorizing', *International Organization*, 24 (Spring 1970), pp. 618–39.
19. Ernst Haas and Philippe Schmitter, 'Economics and Differential Patterns of Political Integration' in *International Political Communities* (New York: Doubleday, 1966), pp. 259–300; Leon Linbdberg, *The Political Dynamics of European Economic Integration* (Stanford: Stanford University Press, 1963).
20. Leon Lindberg and Stuart Scheingold, *Europe's Would-be Polity: Patterns of Change in the European Community* (Englewood Cliffs, N.J.: Prentice-Hall, 1970), pp. 134–8.

21. Ernst Haas, *The Obsolescence of Regional Integration Theory* (Berkeley: Institute of International Studies of the University of California, 1975), pp. 32–40.
22. Robert Keohane and Joseph Nye, *Transnational Relations and World Politics* (Cambridge, MA: Harvard University Press, 1973), pp. ix–xxix.
23. Stanley Hoffmann, 'Obstinate or Obsolete? The Fate of the Nation-State and the Case of Western Europe', *Daedalus*, 95 (Summer 1966), pp. 862–905.
24. Haas, *Obsolescence of Regional Integration Theory*, pp 15–39.
25. Ibid., pp. 86–91.
26. Oran Young, 'Interdependence in World Politics', *International Journal*, 24 (Spring 1969), p. 726.
27. Fred Greenstein and Nelson Polsby, 'International Politics' in *Handbook of Political Science*, vol. 8 (Reading, MA: Addison-Wesley Publishing Company, 1975), pp. 340–95.
28. Ibid., p. 371.
29. R. R. Kaufman, H. I. Chernots and D. S. Geller, 'Preliminary Test of the Theory of Dependency', *Comparative Politics*, 7 (April 1975), pp. 303–30.
30. 'One and Two Don't Make Three', *The Economist*, 9 March 1985), p. 50.
31. Paul Taylor, *The Limits of European Integration* (New York: Columbia University Press, 1983), p. 302.
32. Ibid., p. 307.
33. Robert O. Keohane and Joseph S. Nye, *Power and Interdependence* (Boston: Little, Brown and Company, 1977).
34. Ibid., p. 34 (emphasis in original).
35. Ibid., p. 13.
36. Ibid., p. 36.
37. Grant Hugo, *Appearance and Reality in International Relations* (New York: Columbia University Press, 1970).
38. Keohane and Nye, *Power and Interdependence*, p. 19.
39. 'Arms Procurement', *Debates of the European Parliament*, 11 October 1983, no. 1–304, pp. 53–76.
40. 'A Hint of Progress at Last', *The Economist*, 27 October 1984, p. 54.
41. 'Madrid and Lisbon: New hurdle to market entry', *New York Times*, 5 December 1984, p. 1.
42. Haas, 'The Study of Regional Integration', pp. 11–12.
43. Ibid., p. 31.

1 The division of sovereignty

The termination of World War Two ushered in an era denominated by the emergence of the United States as a global power and the division and realignment of Europe into competing blocs. While not immediately apparent, the seeds of diversity were then being sown, some at random and some preordained by the course of events. While the status and shape of Europe were still open to question, the patent global primacy of the United States was merely a matter of time, will and national objective. Political, economic and security issues, discrete except for the war years, were again separated as rebuilding and reassertion of loyalties commenced. But the shape and manner of international politics had changed so as no longer to allow the clarity that such discreteness required. Recognition of these modifications was slow in coming, requiring, as it did, changes both internal and external to prevailing state systems. Although precise dates and changes are open to discussion it is clear that three periods in post war Europe together may account for the present dynamics evident in both intra-European and American–European relations.

FROM CHAOS TO COMMUNITY: 1945–58

The desire on the part of the United States to return to its isolationist posture of non-commitment was quickly dismissed by the course of European events. The United States emerged from the war with its industrial, political and social base untouched and primed for the transition to meet pent-up post-war domestic needs. Although tensions between the United States and the Soviet Union continued, American demobilization of its European troops was unaffected, with total force structures reduced by 75 per cent in less than one year.[1] Public demand and the difficulties of transitioning to a peacetime stance required that the American military presence in Europe be kept at a minimum and be primarily orientated to the administration of German occupation. To offset what Secretary of Defense Forrestal termed the 'predominance of Soviet land power in Europe' were the factors of American sea power, sole possession of the atomic bomb and the superior, although latent, production capability of the United States industrial infrastructure.[2] George Kennan soon provided the theoretical framework for the American posture toward the Soviet Union in the terms of containment and its later operational translation into the concept of massive retaliation.[3]

While conceptually complete, the inadequacy of the American military forces left both containment and later deterrence devoid of immediate foreign policy coherence. The commitment of the Truman administration to trim defence costs in favour of domestic spending merely underscored the inadequacy of the post-war American guarantees to Europe. Thus the 1947 Truman Doctrine pledging American assistance to Greece and Turkey was in practice a shift in both attitude and in commitment toward implementing the vague formulas defined by containment.[4] The first public appraisal of the need to augment American force capabilities consistent with containment was the publication of NSC–68 in April 1950.[5] Even though NSC–68 called for an across the board military build-up to ensure the ability to address hostilities at all levels, it still remained at odds with the prevailing budget posture of the Truman administration.

The prospects of a long drawn-out debate between defence and domestic spending was cut short by the outbreak of the Korean conflict in 1950. Unsure whether hostilities were local in nature or instead signalled the advent of global Soviet action, the Truman administration decided in favour of the NSC–68 recommendations and increased defence spending from $13 billion in fiscal 1950 to $50.4 billion by fiscal 1954.[6] While prosecuting the war in Korea the United States also began what became a continuous presence in Western Europe by revitalizing the 1949 NATO treaty with the stationing of eight American divisions in that operational theatre. Although these NATO force requirements established at the 1952 Lisbon Conference were later drastically reduced, the legacy of the Korean conflict was a permanent and major American military commitment to European defence and security.[7]

The aftermath of Korea again saw a desire to cut defence costs and commitments, but within the now defined agreement to protect Europe. This objective of an inexpensive but credible defence posture became the foundation for the New Look strategy of the Eisenhower administration.[8] Essentially the New Look relied on nuclear weapons, because they were cost-effective and in the sole possession of the United States, to back conventional forces in Europe as well as to minimize domestic defence expenditures. Simultaneously, the United States expanded the concept of containment by encircling the Soviet Union with a web of regional alliances all grounded on the American nuclear monopoly. Although the assessments of the New Look had to be altered when the Soviet Union gained possession of a credible nuclear response, the tenets of containment and massive retaliation continued as the foundation of American policy throughout the 1950s.

While this American assessment of the military threat posed by the Soviet Union to Europe only emerged over a period of years, the recognition of the need to help Europe rebuild, both economically and socially, was clearer and more coherent in its dimensions. The partition of Europe and the coups in Czechoslovakia and Hungary made it clear to successive American administrations that the major threat to European stability was internal rather than external in its dimensions. Whether viewed as an altruistic act or instead as a pragmatic assessment consistent with the desire to remain free of permanent European entanglements, the introduction of the Marshall Plan emerges as a starting point for the revitalization of Europe. A total of $577 million was channelled to West European governments with the express purpose of rebuilding the economy, restoring the social fabric and creating a Europe that could serve as an ally rather than merely a dependant of the United States.[9] The Marshall Plan was augmented by American efforts to re-establish the global economic system through the Bretton Woods agreement for monetary policy and the General Agreement on Tariffs and Trade (GATT) for trade and commercial activities. Thus not only was Europe provided with the means to rebuild itself, but a framework within which that progress could be implemented was also established. With the dollar serving as the international reserve currency and trade barriers being dismantled by the Dillon Round of the GATT, the Western economies began their progress toward greater interdependence, but always based on the acknowledged primacy of the United States. Although substantial in its impact, it was also apparent that Marshall Plan funds alone would be incapable of meeting the demands of the European economies. While political stabilization and meeting the needs of the populace were short-term objectives, longer-range goals had to include the reorientation of European industrial capabilities in line with the dictates of the emerging post-war economic environment. While the West German infrastructure was in many ways still intact, those of France and the United Kingdom required major infusions of both capital and resources.[10] It was the combination of this demand coupled with the excess production capability of the American economy that prompted the influx of its multinational enterprises (MNEs) into Western Europe in the early 1950s.[11] Bringing with them jobs, resources and 'know-how', American firms quickly established themselves as a principal economic force in most Western European states. National firms, even after rebuilding and with massive infusions of state funds and preferences, were still hard pressed to compete with American firms even within their own domestic market areas. The outcome was ever greater reliance on American managerial experience and competence as Europe sought to shed its status as a junior partner to the United States. Thus in the maintenance of both the external politico-military environment, as well as in the internal European production and supply of goods, the United States remained dominant.

Although more limited in their options, European states, after emerging from the instability of the immediate post-war years, began to define their future roles in this global order grounded on American leadership. Secure in the knowledge that the external environment would be stabilized by the United States, Europeans began to focus on refining relationships within their newly defined borders. Militarily there was no question but that prime reliance had to remain on American forces and their attendant nuclear guarantees. Instead the defence issue centred on how best to rationalize the European contribution to the allied effort. Although the NATO treaty was signed in 1949, it was not until 1954 that it became the primary institution charged with the defence of Western Europe. The essential difficulty was the manner by which the West Germans, potentially the largest European contributor to NATO, would be accommodated within any Allied security arrangement. Initial French reluctance to allow a standing German army within NATO led to the alternative of a proposed European Defence Community (EDC), which would allow German participation without the necessity of a permanent national army. Although strongly supported by the United States, the EDC ultimately failed because of a negative vote in 1954 by the French National Assembly where both right and left joined to defeat the measure.[12] The defeat of a plan that would have allowed European defence and related security issues to be defined and implemented within one institutional forum effected the split that remains to date. The result is that the United States still plays the leading role in those issues of defence and security which should instead be of primarily European concern. Concurrent with this re-evaluation of the NATO agreement was the signing of the Western European Union (WEU) treaty by the six major European states. Although secondary to NATO, because of the lack of American participation, the WEU agreement's automatic response in case of attack on a member provided a European sense to security issues lacking in these NATO arrangements.[13]

Consistent with efforts to define a European role in defence and security were measures to coordinate economic and perhaps political structures pursuant to the re-emergence of Europe. While initial efforts to secure peace through the elimination of state boundaries were destined to flounder on national pride, selective measures to strengthen Europe were successfully implemented through the 1952 establishment of the European Coal and Steel Community (ECSC). Initially agreed by France and West Germany, the ECSC was soon extended to include the Benelux states as well as Italy. The formula whereby France gained German resources in exchange for imparting a sense of legitimacy to the previous foe was thereby established. The same six states eventually extended their cooperation by the end of the 1950s with the formation of Euratom and the European Economic Community (EEC) or Common Market.

THE DEMISE OF AMERICAN MILITARY AND ECONOMIC DOMINANCE: 1959–73

The foreign policy views of the Kennedy administration ensured an immediate change from the more passive dictates of containment and massive retaliation to the active pursuit of programmes to meet and challenge global Soviet adventurism. This foreign policy activism required a restructuring of American forces to meet a two-and-a-half war contingency, including the development of smaller units to deal with counterinsurgency and unconventional warfare. Consistent with this objective, American strategic doctrine was changed from massive retaliation to flexible response, with its goal of 'assured destruction' made possible by a graduated and nuanced use of force according to the nature of the threat.[14] Although Kennedy's commitment to European defence was publicized in his Berlin speech, most of the attention of the new administration was on the more romantic action to be prosecuted against guerrilla movements now springing up globally. The desire to be able to meet aggression wherever and at whatever level it occurred assured a primacy to the building up of conventional forces largely neglected under the New Look's reliance on massive retaliation. Whether caused by the existence of forces to undertake such action or due to more concrete and long-range American foreign policy goals, Kennedy now intensified the American involvement that was to lead to the ten-year-long prosecution of the war in Vietnam. By 1968 defence spending had risen to $78 billion, $20 billion of which was directly used to finance the fighting in Vietnam.[15]

Although the Vietnam conflict lasted until 1975, it was apparent by

1969 that a fundamental reappraisal of American security policy and attendant global commitments was needed. Prior assessments of the use of nuclear weapons had been grounded on the superiority of American weapons and delivery systems, imparting credibility to the European guarantee that was ultimately based on the invulnerability of the United States homeland. By the late 1960s the Soviet Union had achieved the ability to inflict an unacceptable level of damage on the United States and this capability could only increase with the passage of time. Thus while overall nuclear force levels still favoured the United States, the Nixon administration now began a two-pronged approach toward the Soviets. Both arms control negotiations and 'détente' were designed to make the Soviet Union aware that it had more to gain by supporting the existing system than by destroying it.[16] Although the results of linkage and détente are still being debated, one constant emerging from the Nixon reassessment was the determination that the defence of Western Europe must remain the principal planning contingency for American forces. Although the United States scaled down its overall force requirements from a two-and-a-half to a one-and-a-half war capability, the American presence in NATO was strengthened. This concern with European defence ensured that the American nuclear guarantee remained credible and was perceived as such by Europeans and Soviets alike.

While American primacy in military matters was still clear, it was in the economic sphere that events coalesced to call into question the ability of the United States unilaterally to maintain the shape of the post-war international system. Following from the 'guns and butter' prosecution of the Vietnam conflict the inflation rate in the United States soon reached unacceptable levels.[17] An immediate outcome was the instability of the dollar which, although still backed by gold, continued to lose much of its value against major European currencies. In order for the dollar to be allowed to find its own exchange level President Nixon opted on 15 August 1971 to allow the American currency no longer to be convertible into gold.[18] The dollar was now backed solely by the strength and vitality of the American economy, the future of which was increasingly uncertain.

Europeans were in a dilemma with respect to how to address the floating dollar. Given the vast quantities of dollars held in their reserves any effort to diminish its value would also serve to lessen the worth of their holdings. But to continue to support the dollar would serve to increase the cost of their own currencies to the detriment of export-related transactions. In the absence of a single European currency that could serve to supplant the trade role of the dollar, most European governments opted to support the dollar and offset their currency devaluations for export trade through direct subsidies to domestic firms.

The ability to structure these *ad hoc* responses to the dollar crisis was terminated by the OPEC oil crisis with its fourfold rise in oil prices and the ensuing global recession as states sought additional revenues to finance oil imports. Because oil was still priced in dollars the United States was able to finance imports by deficit spending. European states were not so fortunate. But both the United States and Europe began to question the utility of the post-war international trade system in the face of these monetary and economic shocks. While many of the issues raised by the transfer of funds to the oil-producing states have been resolved with time, the essential question, that of the shape of any new system to replace Bretton Woods and similar arrangements, is still in the process of resolution.

For Europeans the inability of the United States unilaterally to maintain the shape of the post-war environment came as both a challenge and as a source of concern. While still content to play a secondary role in the defence aspects of the relationship, there was a growing recognition that European and American economic policies might no longer be viewed as complementary and perhaps had even progressed to the point of open competition.

While both partners still recognized the essential interdependence of Western economies, the asymmetries favouring the Americans were no longer viewed as beneficial by Europeans. The focus of the EEC had been to perfect its internal trading area by dismantling many of the obstacles to intraregional sales while simultaneously erecting tariff barriers for goods imported into the region. While effective in limiting American agricultural imports, the fact that many American MNEs had establshed themselves in the region prior to its formal inception allowed them free access to the internal market, particularly in the increasingly important areas of high-technology goods and processes. Thus while the dismantling of the external international system created opportunities for European manufacturers, the fact that primacy in these growth areas was held by American MNEs active in Europe created tensions that remain to date. The accession of the United Kingdom to the EEC in 1973 created a sales area which rivalled that of the United States in terms of capability, although one that still lagged far behind in terms of productivity. While specific Community actions designed to redress this imbalance will be the topic of a later chapter, suffice it to note that it was the active role of American firms in the Community coupled with the inability of the United States unilaterally to maintain the external trading system that has prompted the current reappraisal within Europe.

THE EMERGENCE OF AN INDEPENDENT EUROPEAN IDENTITY SINCE
1974

The challenge to American strategic dominance acknowledged
between 1959 and 1973 was now made explicit as the Soviet Union
achieved the build-up first articulated in the aftermath of the Cuban
Missile Crisis. Vowing never again to be put in a position of having to
'blink first', the Soviet Union surpassed the United States in many of
the key indicators of strategic capability.[19] When added to its already
acknowledged conventional superiority, especially against NATO
forces, it was apparent that the substance of the American guarantee to
defend Western Europe was increasingly open to question. Although
American officials still voiced support for the nuclear umbrella and
stated their willingness to risk destruction in case of attack, the credibility of this pledge was questioned by many Europeans. This
questioning of American commitment was enhanced by what many in
Europe felt were the less than clear signals of the Carter administration
especially when assessing Soviet global intentions.[20] This sense of the
decoupling of Europe from the United States pervaded much of the
relationship between these allies in the mid- to late 1970s. Whether the
build-up of the Reagan administration and the deployment of cruise
and Pershing missiles has recoupled Europe to the United States is a
matter still open to speculation. But the net effect was the discussion,
perhaps really for the first time, of the need for post-war Europe to
regain some, if not most, of the responsibility for its own defence and
security requirements.

This reassessment of the American–European defence relationship
was matched by action in the areas of economic and commercial
policy. As each partner moved from manufacturing into service-related
economies there was a growing recognition that securing market shares
in the new technologies was the key to both international influence
and, more importantly, to the maintenance of domestic standards of
living. The continued domination of these growth sectors by
European-based American firms, when coupled with the fact that the
American economy proved itself the more dynamic in emerging from
the latest round of recession, has merely intensified European fears of
being left behind.

Finally, this period brought to fruition some of the efforts begun
earlier to place Europe in the position of an equal, at least in selected
commercial areas, to the United States. Success in the GATT Tokyo
Round to limit the provisions of the American 'Buy American' Act with
respect to sales of Airbus products in the United States market is but

one example.[21] Of more importance was the 1979 creation of the European Monetary System (EMS), with its basket of currencies, serving as a European stabilizer against erratic dollar exchange rates as well as seeking to merge European economies as a response to changes dictated by evolutions in the international system as a whole.[22] While minor in their immediate impact, the success of these selected cooperative actions presaged their extension into other issue areas.

NOTES

1. Amos Jordan and William Taylor, Jr., *American National Security* (Baltimore: Johns Hopkins University Press, 1981), Chapter 4.
2. Ibid.
3. George Kennan, 'Sources of Soviet Conduct', *Foreign Affairs*, 25 (July 1947), pp. 566–82.
4. 'The Truman Doctrine', *Record*, 80th Cong., 1st sess., pp. 1980–1.
5. Executive Secretary on United States Objectives and Programs for National Security, *NSC-68: A Report to the National Security Council*, 14 April 1950.
6. Jordan and Taylor, *American National Security*, Chapter 4.
7. William Mako, *U.S. Ground Forces and the Defense of Central Europe* (Washington, DC: The Brookings Institution, 1983), pp. 11–12.
8. The Harvard Nuclear Study Group (HNSG), *Living with Nuclear Weapons* (New York: Bantam Books, 1983), pp. 78–82.
9. Alfred Grosser, *The Western Alliance* (New York: Vintage Books, 1982), p. 65.
10. Ibid., p. 34.
11. Joseph Rallo, 'The European Community and the Multinational Enterprise' in Leon Hurwtiz, ed., *The Harmonization of European Public Policy* (Westport, CT: Greenwood Press, 1983), pp. 159–82.
12. Grosser, *The Western Alliance*, pp. 125–8.
13. Assembly of Western European Union, *Thirty Years of the Modified Brussels Treaty*, 30th ordinary session, 1st part, 15 May 1984, Doc. 973.
14. HNSG, *Nuclear Weapons*, pp. 86–90.
15. Jordan and Taylor, *American National Security*, Chapter 4.
16. John Lewis Gaddis, 'The Rise, Fall and Future of Detente', *Foreign Affairs*, 62, 2 (Winter 1983/84), pp. 354–77.
17. *Defense Program and Budget Fiscal Year 1970*. Before House sub-committee on Department of Defense Appropriations, 25 February 1970 (US Government Printing Office, Washington, DC), esp. pp. 13–20.
18. *Trade: U.S. Policy since 1945* (Washington, DC: Congressional Quarterly, Inc., 1984), pp. 73–8.
19. HNSG, *Nuclear Weapons*, p. 90.
20. John Allen Williams, 'Defense Policy: The Carter–Reagan Record', *The Washington Quarterly*, 6, 4 (Autumn 1983), pp. 79–92.
21. Joseph Rallo, 'The European Communities Industrial Policy Revisited: The Case of Aerospace', *Journal of Common Market Studies*, 22, 3 (March 1984), pp. 245–67.
22. Benjamin Cohen, 'The EMS, the Dollar and the Future of the International Monetary System', paper prepared for the Conference on The Political Economy of the European Monetary System, Bologna, Italy, 16–17 November 1979, pp. 1–27.

2 Intra-Alliance sources of tension

While Chapter 1 detailed the general tensions that have engaged the attention of the United States and Western Europe, it is now essential to assess the implications of those recurrent themes. Although the nature of these tensions is manifested in intraregional outcomes, the cause is more comprehensive, finding its antecedents in the general restructuring of the international economic and security environment. While military and security issues remain more constant in their dimensions than do political and economic concerns, their combined effect is to question the total relationship given the increased connection between what were previously viewed as discrete issues and problems. For ease of analysis the following sections will disaggregate the segments of these issues, recognizing though that overlap is central to any analysis and predictive usefulness.

SECURITY: DEFENCE OR DETERRENCE IN WESTERN EUROPE

The nuclear umbrella spread over Western Europe in the aftermath of World War Two was a clear break with the traditional American policy of non-entanglement in foreign, especially European, affairs. Given the potential ramifications of this guarantee there has never been complete certainty within even successive American administrations as to its substance and scope. As long as the American nuclear capability was a monopoly or at least markedly superior to that of the Soviet Union, the need to question the credibility of the guarantee was never reached. With the acknowledgement in SALT I of nuclear parity between the superpowers, the credibility issue now became central to Alliance relations.[1] It was this issue that essentially became the basis for the 1979 NATO 'twin-track' decision and the stimulus for the European demonstrations seeking to counter the intermediate-range nuclear force (INF) deployment.[2] Although credibility was the issue, it was merely indicative of a greater perceptual change about how defence and security in Western Europe were to be accomplished. For an understanding of the ramifications of that change it is necessary briefly to review American policy toward NATO and the latter's role in the larger issue of global security arrangements.

In the wake of World War Two American defence policy was a reflection of the unsettled and ambivalent assessment of its overall global role. Although acknowledging its undisputed global military and economic primacy, the traditional theme of isolationism or perhaps simple reticence made it difficult for the United States easily to assume that role. Military demobilization occurred at an un-precedented rate as ground forces in the European theatre dropped from sixty-nine divisions to only one by 1950.[3] The adherence of the Truman administration to a balanced budget assured that spending would be channelled so as to pursue the domestic transition back to a peacetime economy rather than to enhance the American defence effort. While not turning his back on the needs of Europe it was clear that Truman did not immediately view continued participation in Europe as vital to developing American security needs. But events in Eastern Europe quickly made it apparent that some form of American presence in Europe was needed. The massive but economically directed assistance of the 1947 Truman Doctrine and the 1948 Marshall Plan was consistent with the prevailing view that such programmes were short-term and designed to re-establish Europe's ability to rebuild in a manner that would prove consistent with, and congenial to, American foreign policy objectives. Although NATO was established in 1949, it was really the outbreak of the Korean conflict and the uncertainty over Soviet global intentions that lastingly altered the American position on Europe.

Although finally recognizing the need to maintain an American presence in Europe, this commitment was still defined by domestic budgetary constraints rather than by the nature of the potential threat across the inner-German border.[4] While permanent American forces were established in Europe by 1950, the primary security guarantee was firmly grounded on the nuclear monopoly held by the United States. Additionally, the inability of the Soviet Union to inflict any measure of damage on the American homeland imbued this policy with a sense of invulnerability and independence perhaps unique in the post-war era. This formula of ground-based American forces serving as a 'trip-wire' to trigger a nuclear response thus became the basis for the United States' defence of Europe from the threat of external aggression.

The New Look of the Eisenhower administration continued this formula even as it sought to rework American force capabilities to undertake broader tasks in support of enhanced global security commitments. The first major post-war statement on the American commitment to Europe was NSC-68, released in 1950, which recommended substantial force increases more consistent with the nature of the evolving Soviet threat. Integral to NSC-68 was its assessment that the Soviet Union would not achieve a usable nuclear capability until 1954, at which time the American monopoly and the sanctity of the homeland, with their attendant policy ramifications, would have to be rethought. Although NSC-68 assumed a breathing space of a few years before any major Soviet assertion of power might be anticipated the events of the Korean conflict belied that conclusion.

Korea caused a match between the military assessments of NSC-68 and the political objectives of Kennan's containment in furtherance of a credible American foreign policy. This new posture toward Europe was now to be backed by the presence of substantial ground forces as well as the threat of massive retaliation through the employment of nuclear weapons. While it was not entirely credible that Soviet activity anywhere in the world would be punished by nuclear means, the primacy of the American arsenal ensured that the question need not be asked. But increasingly the nature of Soviet actions in Hungary and the dismay occasioned by the 1957 launch of the Sputnik began to reshape American thoughts on the size and purpose of the defence budget. Now the nature of the threat rather than its cost began to be viewed as the prime determinant in defence outlays. While defence expenditure did not grow appreciably in the 1950s, the need to rethink those small budget outlays did become apparent.

The first defence pronouncement of the Kennedy administration reflected this new attitude on the primacy of defence in American foreign policy. While budgets were debated the need to imbue American security policy with a more credible capability was reflected in the doctrinal change from massive retaliation to flexible response. No longer relying solely on nuclear weapons, American doctrine would now be based on a panoply of assets ranging from unconventional to strategic nuclear weapons. In keeping with this manifested increase in capabilities was the willingness to use all military assets to fulfil the objectives of containment. The net result of capability and will was the American involvement in Vietnam.

Although Vietnam had no direct impact on Europe the indirect fallout soon became apparent. American NATO forces were denuded of personnel and material so as to supply troop requirements in Vietnam. Unlike Korea, where several NATO allies sent forces, none did to Vietnam, reflecting an uneasiness with this new and increasingly aggressive American security posture.[5] Although American defence spending rose during the period of the Vietnam conflict the effect on forces not directly involved in that fighting was generally negative. Training and material requirements were keyed to jungle-type warfare and not to the very different needs of the NATO fronts. It was only in the wind-down from Vietnam under the Nixon administration that American NATO forces could begin to recoup some of their losses and regain their sense of primacy in the American scheme of global security arrangements.

The security reassessment of the Nixon administration took into consideration the prestige loss and narrowed global perspective resulting from the Vietnam experience. Détente and linkage were the political corollaries to the Nixon Doctrine which expressly limited the use of American forces in most regional conflicts.[6] SALT I legitimized parity between the superpowers by acknowledging a balance in their strategic inventories. Although conventional superiority in Europe still rested with the Warsaw Pact, it was held to be manageable given the political effort made to draw the Soviet Union into the prevailing international system within the tenets of détente.

Europeans also enjoyed this seeming thaw as *Ostpolitik* and the Helsinki accords sought to make certain what until that time had seemed enviable goals. While the oil crisis and its attendant economic disruptions did have an impact on military matters, principally by increasing energy-related expenses, they too were deemed acceptable in the political context of the period. Overriding any sense of conventional force inferiority was reliance on the concept of deterrence, codified by the ABM portion of SALT I, that held American and Soviet cities hostage to any aggressive acts on the part of either superpower. But even this uneasy balance was questioned in the mid-1970s and finally undone by events later in that decade.

While there can be no precise dates and events that precipitated the reassessment of the strategic balance late in the 1970s, it is apparent that one of the factors responsible for a shift in American attitudes was a change in the perception of Soviet intentions. An unwritten assumption of détente was that once military equality had been achieved between both powers, each would seek to remain at that level, thus minimizing the need to engage anew in a costly and destabilizing arms race. It became increasingly apparent by the late 1970s that this was not the Soviet intention as its strategic and conventional forces continued to build up at a rate unprecedented during peacetime. Whether this Soviet action was the result of internal bureaucratic pressures or instead a response to their view of the external environment is less important than the rethinking that it occasioned in the West. While the Soviet build-up had not, as yet, threatened the capability of the United States to respond with nuclear force, this was not the case with respect to the Alliance perception of that threat. West German Chancellor Schmidt, among others, began to question the American nuclear guarantees to Europe and focused on the lack of any operational gradations between conventional and strategic types of weapons.[7] The essence of the concern was the question whether, in response to a limited conventional Soviet incursion into Western Europe, the United States would risk destruction of its own forces and homeland by responding with strategic weapons. When combined with increased Soviet military activity, culminating in the 1979 invasion of Afghanistan, even the relatively passive views of President Carter took a startling change in direction. While the 1980 presidential campaign focused on the more ephemeral issue of personal competency the election of Mr Reagan signalled a major change in American security policy and outlook.[8] This change was dramatically acknowledged in the 1986 BA annual defence appropriations budget, particularly in outlays for areas such as personnel, operations/maintenance and procurement (Table 1). Once again ideological confrontation backed by increasingly capable military assets became the centrepiece of American security policy. While strategic nuclear assets were increased, so too was the ability to wage war at less than an all-out level. Although American incursions into Lebanon, Grenada and Central America must not be equated with Vietnam or even Korea, the assumptions underlying the use of power shared many similarities with those earlier events and periods.

For Western Europe this about-turn on the part of the United States was simultaneously frightening and reassuring. The NATO 'twin-track' decision gain seemed to couple American and European defence by placing at risk both homelands if these intermediate nuclear weapons were ever utilized.[9] Thus both perceptions of credibility and the presence of capability were reassuring to Europeans who still viewed the United States as the linchpin of their security arrangements. But at the same time there was an increased feeling of alarm as this American presence was viewed in yet another dimension.

For the West deterrence signified that one promised unacceptable levels of damage if attacked yet nullified the ability to protect one's homeland or society from initial attack and perhaps destruction. This mutual hostage situation was the key to ensuring that war never occurred. But the build-up of Soviet forces began to make clear that this definition of deterrence was not shared in the East. The Soviet definition of deterrence differed and implied that hostilities would best be averted by having forces sufficient to wage and win a war if one ever broke out. Only if Soviet force build-ups were analysed according to this war-winning definition did their composition and size make any sense.[10]

What now concerns Europeans is the increasing realization that the

United States is also subscribing to this war-winning scenario, even at the expense of lessening the Alliance commitment to deterrence. The MX, B-1 and cruise missile, as well as the Strategic Defense Initiative (SDI), are all viewed as moving American force structures and operational capabilities toward this objective. The European concern is easily understood if one remembers that the battlefield under either scenario remains the same. Thus while the ability to deter by the capacity to win might actually be more credible, its failure still results in the destruction of Western Europe. The 1984 statements of Henry Kissinger on the need to restructure NATO in keeping with a movement toward a war-fighting capacity did little to assuage European fears.[11] The proposed Nunn Amendment, calling for a reduction of American NATO-based forces, was similarly met with mixed feelings, given the absence of any coordinated European response that could assume those responsibilities.[12]

Three current American initiatives on the manner of waging war in Europe have emerged as particularly troublesome to European NATO members because their existence seems to signal, in an operational sense, a dramatic departure from the tenets of deterrence theory. The most controversial of the three programmes is the Strategic Defense Initiative (SDI) announced by President Reagan on 23 March 1983.[13] Although focused on the concept of strategic deterrence, SDI's umbrella is also viewed as an adjunct to a conventional non-nuclear defence of Europe. It is this latter aspect, raising the prospect of the superpowers testing each other free from worry about nuclear escalation, that has proved unacceptable to substantial segments of Europe's population. While this public attention has been focused on the increased likelihood of war, government leaders, especially in France and Britain, have instead been concerned with the potential deterioration of their own limited strategic systems under an SDI umbrella. It is an article of faith in European government circles that the Soviet Union will match this new American capability through their own system or by dramatically increasing their strategic assets in order to overwhelm through sheer numbers the various SDI layers. In either case French and British arsenals, being modernized at great cost, would lose much if not all of their foreign policy implications.[14] Inferred, but not explicitly stated, is the fear that the possession of SDI systems by only the United States and the Soviet Union would create a new global hierarchy excluding Europe and further intensifying its slide to secondary power status. It is for these reasons that President Mitterrand has called for a moratorium on space-based systems until negotiations might be concluded on how best to direct progress on the use of any such programmes.[15]

Table 1. Department of Defense—B/A Appropriation (millions of dollars)

	FY 1976	FY 1980	FY 1982	FY 1983	FY 1984	FY 1985	FY 1986
Current Dollars							
Military Personnel	25,430	31,014	42,875	45,688	64,866[a]	68,901[a]	73,425[a]
Retired Pay	7,326	11,965	14,986	16,155			
Operation & Maintenance	28,731	46,365	62,466	66,540	70,950	78,219	82,450
Procurement	20,991	35,283	64,462	80,355	86,161	96,807	106,813
Research, Development, Test & Evaluation	9,451	13,561	20,060	22,798	26,867	31,464	39,280
Special Foreign Currency Programme	3	7	3	4	3	9	2
Military Construction	2,360	2,293	4,916	4,512	4,510	5,517	7,057
Family Housing & Homeowners Assistance Programme	1,229	1,526	2,203	2,712	2,669	2,894	3,283
Revolving & Management Funds	135	1,336	2,494	1,075	2,774	1,554	1,860
Trust Funds, Receipts & Deductions	−146	−727	−714	−365	−650	−636	−659
Proposed Legislation							189
Total · Direct Programme (B/A)	95,508	142,621	213,751	239,474	258,150	284,730	313,700

Constant FY 1986 Dollars

Military Personnel	50,727	48,045	50,567	51,803	70,701[a]	72,519[a]	73,425[a]
Retired Pay	13,645	16,127	17,044	17,368			
Operation & Maintenance	53,005	57,962	68,595	70,927	74,554	79,513	82,450
Procurement	44,402	50,643	79,061	93,211	95,070	101,611	106,813
Research, Development, Test & Evaluation	17,409	18,203	23,356	25,567	29,056	32,717	39,280
Special Foreign Currency Programme	5	9	4	4	3	9	2
Military Construction	-4,326	2,969	5,756	5,076	4,872	5,724	7,057
Family Housing & Homeowners Assistance Programme	2,283	2,067	2,489	3,023	2,879	3,010	3,283
Revolving & Management Funds	261	1,876	2,945	1,234	3,045	1,649	1,860
Trust Funds, Receipts & Deductions	-272	-979	-807	-397	-680	-641	-659
Proposed Legislation							189
Total · Direct Programme (B/A)	185,791	196,922	249,009	267,817	279,501	296,111	313,700

Note: Totals may not add due to rounding.

[a] Includes Retired Pay Accrual.

Source: Report of the Secretary of Defense to the Congress, *FY1986 Budget, FY1987 Authorization Request and FY1986–1990 Defense Programs*, 4 February 1985, p. 293.

The second American initiative creating concern in Europe was the 1983 deployment of intermediate-range nuclear forces (INF) in several European NATO states.[16] The deployment was prompted initially by West German Chancellor Schmidt's concern over an imbalance in Europe which could operationally negate NATO's flexible response doctrine since there were no effective systems between the conventional and the strategic levels capable of matching the Soviet SS-20s arrayed against Western Europe. After protracted negotiations, NATO agreed to INF deployment based on what came to be termed the 'twin-track' policy. Briefly stated, NATO would deploy INF assets in late December 1983 only if negotiations failed to convince the Soviet Union to withdraw its SS-20s from the European operational area. Although controversy over possible agreement from the 'walk in the woods' dialogue continues, the Soviet refusal to withdraw their missiles prompted NATO to follow through on its deployment promise.[17] Although Belgium and the Netherlands continued to vacillate over deployment of their share of INF systems, cruise and Pershing IIs were placed in the UK, Italy and West Germany by the middle of 1984.

Public opposition to INF deployment, although reaching its zenith in the fall of 1983, continued to have significant ramifications even after that date. While demonstrations at Greenham Common and elsewhere attracted the bulk of media attention it was in the acceptance of these views at elite levels that long-term policy implications became manifest. In particular the British Labour Party's anti-deployment platform and the West German SPD's break with its former leader Helmut Schmidt, remain submerged yet potentially volatile problems given the party shifts traditional in European national elections.[18]

Although INF deployment was based on the operational requirements of flexible response it has been the associated credibility issue, addressed under the rubric of 'coupling', that has emerged as a major source of intra-Alliance tension. While most Europeans are sanguine about the apparent American evolution to a war-fighting posture they still remain supportive of a balance where the nuclear threshold is at a level sufficient to deter yet within the limits of credibility of response. It is this latter factor that sustained European support for that 1983 deployment decision. But the perception of the nature of the American security guarantee still remains a source of controversy. For underlying that guarantee is the sense of American willingness to risk destruction in support of its allies. While the presence of American forces in Europe is important, it is the perceived willingness to risk national assets that makes the visible commitment credible. Recent American–European foreign policy disagreements have done little to reinforce the NATO position of coupling notwithstanding the actual presence of systems capable of carrying out that promise.

The final American security initiative directed at Europe concerns the role and capability of conventional weapons to deter a Warsaw Pact attack. A rethinking of NATO doctrine to make use of emerging technologies (ETs) and 'deep interdiction' against attacking forces has accompanied the general American desire to increase the ability to defend Europe without the need to resort to nuclear weapons.[19] The European response to this initiative has been somewhat quixotic. Specifically the desirability of eliminating the need for nuclear warfare has been effectively negated by the excessive cost and enhanced usability of these new systems. Additionally the ability of effecting this new operational policy toward a Warsaw Pact attack has yet to be agreed on even at relevant military levels.[20]

In summary, one might conclude that this European tentativeness to support these American initiatives stems not only from uncertainty over their relationship to deterrence but is also due to the absence of any organizational alternative that could merge European capabilities and thus lessen dependence and reliance on United States leadership.

POLITICS: DÉTENTE OR CONTAINMENT

While relations between the Soviet Union, Western Europe and the United States encompass three distinct actors, analyses have generally been collapsed into an East–West dimension. Whether characterized by terms such as containment, linkage or détente, it has become clear of late that American and European assumptions about the substance of those relationships do not precisely overlap.[21] When it is recognized that this Alliance diversity is also carried into intra-European affairs it becomes apparent that one much search for the assumptions that underlie the terms before any prescriptions on the future of these East–West and Alliance relations might be attempted.

While sensitive to the time frame several themes remain consistent and serve to account for persistent differences in American and Western European attitudes toward the Soviet Union. Basic to this discussion is the geographic proximity of Western Europe to the Soviet Union. While the location of West Germany is militarily important, geography also shades into the economic and social context given the national ties that were fragmented in the aftermath of World War Two. Just as it makes economic sense for Toronto to trade with Detroit rather than Vancouver, so too the natural partners of many European states lie directly across an artificial but very real border. While acquiescence to Soviet demands need not follow from this proximity it is clear that Europeans, unlike many Americans, recognize the need for accommodation on a level well below that of mutual antagonism.

As central to the European position as geographical proximity are the priorities expressed by their national budgets.[22] Taxed at a higher rate than their American counterparts, Europeans assume that such funds are used to finance a widespread and increasingly pervasive system of social benefits. Without addressing the equity of such an orientation, its acceptance as a given by both citizen and government assures its primacy when budget allocations are being negotiated. Except for brief periods in the 1960s, budgetary constraints have been imposed by sluggish economies or by expanding social demands on available resources to offset employment shifts created by the emergence of competition at international economic levels. Finite resources and an acknowledged 7:1 ratio in social to defence spending have therefore intervened to colour the perception of the threat posed by the Soviet Union to Europe.[23] Thus while the United States might at times assume unlimited resources to meet a Soviet threat, in Gaddis's terms by adopting a 'symmetrical response', that latitude is not available as an option to European states.[24] Any greater response requires either increased reliance on the United States or more efficiency in allocation of spending, perhaps through aggregation of European capabilities. While the former response has been the norm it is the latter option that is increasingly being viewed as the more palatable.

The final consistent theme is the European reliance on the United States to maintain its security commitments including any Alliance shortfalls due to budgetary or social constraints. The role of primary alliance partner carries with it the burden of willingness, if necessary, to assume most of the shared commitment if other partners are either unwilling or unable to fulfil their roles. When American global primacy was unquestioned even lapses in budgetary commitment under the Nixon Doctrine and the Carter administration did little to shake this tendency to look first to the United States. But of late changes in European attitudes have been reflected in subtle shifts in the American commitment to these open-ended guarantees to Europe. While the Nunn Amendment and the Kissinger Proposals for NATO were analysed not as prescriptions but rather as American prods to reinvigorate NATO they proved far more disturbing to Europeans. Both those who support a continued commitment to NATO and those who seek a greater European independence in shared defence and security matters agreed that these signals were more than academic in their objective. Instead the divergence between the American and European positions that surfaced in the aftermath of the demise of détente now became more focused with the possibility of a major American security reorientation without a plausible European replacement.

Indeed it was the era of détente that brought to the surface many areas of disquiet that had been papered over in the glow of rebuilding Europe and in the activity associated with perfecting the customs and economic market throughout the 1950s and 1960s. Détente, although clearly viewed as an updated form of containment by Kissinger, was instead seen by many Americans and Europeans as dismissing the systemic differences between themselves and the Soviets in support of an overlapping global perspective. Détente signalled to many Europeans that it was now permissible to follow through on commercial, economic and social patterns that had been disrupted by the cold war. *Ostpolitik* was but one of these outcomes. The increase of ties to the East was seen as reflecting consistent European sentiment as well as being a more rational approach to conflict management between the blocks. Trade, always present, now flourished with implications that were not to be manifested completely until détente was officially repudiated.

Interdependence now began to replace polar politics whether as an outcome of, or in coincidence with, détente. While interdependence could manifest itself between equal and unequal partners, detrimental effects were generally defined in North–South rather than East–West or even West–West terms. In the West–West relationship interdependence was felt to be one step toward merging these separate economies in a fashion consistent with the converging political-economic outlook of participating states. The potential asymmetries created by concurrent East–West imbalances were largely ignored in pursuit of the complementarities of Western policies.

By the late 1970s it became apparent that cooperative competition rather than complementarity was becoming the hallmark of West–West relations, manifesting itself particularly in the areas of foreign policy outlooks. The elections of Reagan, Thatcher, Mitterrand and Craxi inaugurated a series of questions concerning Alliance and intra-European foreign policies which might result from the mixture of conservative and socialist leadership that these personalities represented. Ironically the coincidence of their views on security matters as exemplified by support for INF and participation in the 1983 Lebanese peace-keeping force has often been overshadowed by acrimony over the lesser politics of economic relations. The gas pipeline, technology transfers and agricultural supports have tended to dominate the Alliance agenda to an extent that a reappraisal of the apparent equanimity in security matters appears necessary. Does apparent agreement over security matters establish the parameters within which economic debate may occur, or does economic disagreement presage a change in the security outlook and seeming coincidence of views of Alliance members?[25] Phrased differently, does the absence of issue hierarchy in a complex interdependent environment negate the ability to assume discreteness between issue levels, minimizing the directional strength imposed by a more ordered taxonomy? In summary, which aspects of Alliance relations would appear more useful in a predictive sense to assess ramifications throughout the spectrum of foreign policy relations?

Perhaps the clearest statement of the European desire to find an institutional vehicle within which to coordinate and thus enhance foreign policy commonality has been the process termed European Political Cooperation (EPC).[26] Since 1970 EPC has met to coordinate foreign policies on issues central to the Community but deemed outside its permissible mandate for discussion. Although not originally designed to address defence and related security matters, EPC has assumed that role as these issues have become more visible and some manner of coordinated resolution more essential. Although treading a delicate line in order to take account of varying member perspectives on enhancement of security cooperation, EPC signals a European desire to influence Alliance relations through a more direct ability to manage the content and direction of agenda deliberations. In addition to this external function, EPC allows a greater sense of Community coherence and coordination to emerge given its position parallel to existing Community deliberative venues. Although the merger of EPC and Community foreign policy roles is a long-term probability, the short-term outcome is the ability to articulate Alliance foreign policy differences in a manner more supportive of European objectives. EPC has allowed intra-European perspectives on the legitimacy of an East–West overlay on American actions in Central America to have greater impact on the unilaterally determined actions pursued by the current Reagan administration.

ECONOMICS: TRADE WAR OR COOPERATIVE COMPETITION

Perhaps nowhere else is the current tension between the United States and Western Europe manifested more clearly than in the area of commercial, trade and economic relations. The recipients of the Marshall Plan, passive in their dependency, have become active competitors with their former benefactors. While certain traditional European rivalries were minimized with the 1957 signing of the Rome

Treaty, less than spectacular economic growth rates have diminished or made less relevant these earlier agreements. Thus trade and economic competition must be viewed on two distinct but related levels: first, the recognition that American and European economic and commercial objectives no longer precisely overlap and to an increasing extent actually compete; second, the search to develop a European international economic role while moving internally, however gradually, toward the concept of a harmonized commercial, trade and economic Community.

Although glossed over during the economic turmoils of the 1970s the stimulus of American trade competition to the development of the internal Community has been constant and central to many of its earlier successes in the 1950s and 1960s. The 'American Challenge' articulated by Servan-Schreiber in 1966 led directly to the call for more modern management techniques within European firms.[27] Increasingly European states began to merge their firms into what Vernon termed 'national champions', in an effort to address the dominance of the American multinational enterprise (MNE).[28] This effort toward a harmonized European outlook became side-tracked as national priorities began to overwhelm regional cooperation in response to oil-related economic disruptions. National champions, originally viewed as competitive vehicles to address the challenges posed by the international economic system, soon began to be treated as another instrument to protect jobs and ailing domestic industries. While capable of short-term assistance these national subsidies and preferences did little to assist domestic companies in adapting to increasingly competitive global markets. Consistently the protection of jobs meant that national assistance was being channelled, particularly in the United Kingdom, to firms and sectors that were unable to meet the challenge posed by low wage environments in areas such as textiles and steel. The impact on domestic employment and export related capability was manifest and troublesome.

This desire to protect the competitive ability of European firms through national protectionist measures and mergers, although not conducive to the tenets of integration, did at least partially meet the competitive pressures emanating from American firms. Particularly in high-technology sectors, the total number of companies was drastically reduced through nationalization and mergers, ensuring that government assistance was more efficiently utilized by remaining corporate actors.[29] But the competitive challenges of the 1980s are not those of earlier decades. No longer will European firms be able to depend on established market areas built around trade-mark recognition and exports to narrowly defined, often ex-colonial, partners. The patterns of trade have changed and will continue to do so in response to evolutions in the sustaining international economic system.

Western Europe, the United States and Japan are the states in the forefront of the move to service economies. While not losing sight of the fact that many of these jobs will be in low-paying categories, the overriding concern is how that structural shift might change the entire tenor of national industrial policies. No longer will post-war trade relationships define market shares. In this newly evolving system the set of states that can compete to develop and manage these new markets is small and known. The question is how well each member in that set will fare. It is painfully apparent that individual European states recognized their past shortcomings and are now striving to respond to these newer challenges in regionally creative and less nationally dependent terms. It is this recognition that gives substance to current Community initiatives directed at global commercial and economic stature channelled through its industrial policy.[30]

While specific objectives of the Community's industrial policy will be the topic of Chapter 5, certain programmes that shape that initiative are individually important for the themes that they represent. Several particular themes are of central concern. Overarching in importance and presenting in an inchoate sense the opportunity for follow-on measures was the establishment in 1979 of the European Monetary System (EMS).[31] This set out a basket of European currencies as a stabilizing alternative to the erratic dollar for trade, financial and commercial activities.[32] But as the exchange problems caused by a strong dollar demonstrated in 1985, even the EMS is not immune from external pressures. Although the economic consequences of the EMS are important, in allowing Community trade to be denominated in one currency and therefore to be competitive against the dollar or the yen, it is the political underpinning of that system that will be responsible ultimately for its success or failure. The EMS is the first clear sentiment in pursuit of the alternative of a Europe sufficiently united to become, at least in certain sectors, an alternative partner to the United States. The increased acceptance of the EMS as the vehicle by which to denominate and conduct European trade has been translated into practice when pursuing global trade and commercial contacts.

European states and the Community as a whole have assiduously cultivated ties in the developing states based partially on traditional political contacts but increasingly pressing advantages accruing from the EMS to secure outlets for their production of goods and services. While the Lomé Conventions are the most visible manifestations of this relationship, ex-colonial ties also continue to be vigorously exploited.[33]

Whether in the area of arms transfers or for civilian turnkey projects, the share of European trade with the Third World has dramatically escalated over the past few years. The nurturing of ties to these states has been viewed with ambivalence by a Reagan administration whose focus is primarily on traditional East–West dynamics. It is only when European objectives threaten to introduce a third actor to that dyad that concern in the United States surfaces. It is that renewed European sense of the need to engage more actively in global politics that has occupied so much of the foreign policy attention of American administrations in recent years.

Perhaps the most visible of the differing attitudes between the United States and Europe concerning relations with the Soviet Union surfaced in the wake of the gas pipeline issue.[34] European dependence on oil imports from the volatile Middle East spurred the desire to support the building of a pipeline from the Soviet Union to a terminal in West Germany. While several European states would benefit from the source it was the West German government that saw in the venture the answer to several troubling political and economic matters. Consistent with the objectives of *Ostpolitik*, trade credits to finance the pipeline were viewed in more than mere commercial terms. As part of the contract the Soviet Union agreed to purchase pipe from West German firms, a not so subtle inducement to direct aid to a sector severely buffeted by competition from low-wage states.[35] Given the benefits accruing to Europe, the American embargo on pipeline equipment in the wake of the Afghanistan invasion and the later effort to extend these sanctions to Western European firms were viewed as political rather than economic in nature and an additional source of tension between now overtly competitive allies.

The pipeline issue, in turn, mirrored an Alliance problem of longer standing which concerned the sale of high-technology goods to the East. The COCOM Committee exists to oversee the granting of export licences for sensitive goods but the differing American and European definitions of 'stated use' versus 'end use' consistently generated problems over permissible transactions.[36] The fact that Europeans may provide substitutes to most technology embargoed by the United States has resulted in American legislation detailing when embargoes will be utilized in the face of alternative suppliers. These actions have convinced Europeans that much of the American effort was political in nature and therefore it is perfectly acceptable to differ given the increasingly divergent views of how to address East–West relations and contacts. Given this viewpoint the American justification to continue grain sales because they would deplete scarce hard currencies otherwise usable for military purchases was instead seen as furthering

Reagan administration efforts to dictate terms of trade for political ends when deemed necessary by ideologically generated policies.

The final economic topic that relates to intra-Alliance relations, and one that will dominate that agenda for many years, concerns the American offer to Europe to participate in the SDI. Given the political costs associated with even hinting at a direct role in the military aspects of the venture, debate in Europe has centred on how best to respond to the commercial applications of present and contemplated research and development activity. Fear of enlarging the already acknowledged technology gap between Europe and the United States as well as the parallel issues of jobs, sales and revenues, has engaged the current European agenda to an extent rarely seen when an economic issue is the topic. Clearly the possibility of a regionally directed response to the American offer is further clouding the ability of individual European governments to structure their own policy priorities.

NATIONAL BUDGETS: SOCIAL SERVICES OR PEACE THROUGH STRENGTH

Although the attitude of the current American administration on the requisite level of defence spending is clearly triggered by its ideological view of the Soviet threat, that outlook is not, for the most part, shared by its European counterparts. The size, resilience and dynamic qualities of the American economic base allow, even in difficult times, a high level of security spending to be maintained. Gaddis has persuasively argued that the amount of American defence spending is dependent, not on the threat perceived as emanating from the Soviet Union, but rather on an administration's assessment of the means it wishes to make available to counter that threat.[37] Even when there is not a tight correlation between prosperity and defence spending, Gaddis's assertion that domestic factors direct the nature of that response appears sound.

It is no longer possible, if it ever was, to separate spending on social programmes in the United States from security-related expenditures. The interrelationship between commercial and defence contracts held in many instances by only a few firms blurs any attempt at distinction often to the point of meaninglessness. One may though suggest a distinction based on the nature of the appropriation designed to fund defence as opposed to essentially social programmes. Strictly military expenditures centre on personnel and on maintenance costs as well as on weapons procurement, all of which are spread over several years at a relatively fixed rate. Even assuming the cost overruns that have become endemic to the system, these expenditures may be estimated with relative accuracy and thus may be termed fixed. In this manner and assuming a base budget to sustain what are generally agreed as the minimal defence needs and security commitments of the United States, increased spending is generally due to an administration's definition of what new missions are to be performed by the armed forces. American presidents have generally agreed on four basic missions:

(1) to deter nuclear attack on the United States;
(2) to protect European NATO members from Soviet aggression;
(3) to ensure the continuation of oil supplies from the Middle East; and
(4) to maintain the capability to fight a one-half war at any point in the world.[38]

An increase in missions beyond this number is undertaken to accommodate a different perception of the threat by an administration. Thus the two-and-a-half war concept of John F. Kennedy required force increases to wage not only strategic and conventional warfare but also to counter insurgency movements world-wide. In a similar fashion the current Reagan administration has sought to enhance the mission capability of American forces by establishing the Southern Command, with its rapid deployment force, as well as increasing the standard capabilities of the three services across the board. It is this enlargement of basic military missions that is controversial and most likely to come under attack from succeeding administrations or public pressure groups. Decreased defence spending may result from elimination or consolidation of these mission options, yet always within the dictates of long-term fixed programmes and outlays. The designation of non-defence organizations such as NASA to assume militarily related tasks makes a precise accounting of total security directed expenditures even more difficult.

In contrast to the relatively fixed needs of the defence sector are those in the ambit of social spending. While the American definition of 'welfare spending' must not be confused with that prevalent in Western Europe, programmes in both regions seek to provide many of the same benefits. Among these objectives are opportunity grants such as Aid to Families with Dependent Children (AFDC), support for higher education and, naturally, social security. But in contrast to the relatively fixed expenditures for defence, those in the social area are open ended with yearly amounts unknown. Many of these entitlement programmes were developed during the 'Great Society' of President Lyndon B. Johnson and were designed to place more individuals in the mainstream of American society. Individuals became eligible for programme support based on income, family size, inner-city residence and a myriad of other criteria. Even assuming no waste or overlap in the distribution system, the amounts for these programmes have increased dramatically with their outer limits dependent on need rather than on predetermined budget allocations. While it is possible to eliminate or lessen amounts to individuals by adjusting the eligibility criteria, the difficulty of amending the enabling legislation associated with each programme has made this difficult. The demonstrated need for these programmes coupled with an increase in election registration by persons receiving such assistance has enhanced the political costs associated with cutting such expenditures. Even President Reagan's 'New Federalism', which sought to increase state control over eligibility requirements, failed to achieve the politically damaging act of cutting back on benefits.

The second Reagan administration has continued on the path of increasing both the missions to be performed by American forces and the funds directed to defence programmes (amounts for fiscal 1985 are given in Figure 1). Continued activity in Central America, INF deployments and readiness exercises throughout the world account for much of this increase. Even after cutting costs for personnel and maintenance and stretching out the payment programmes for major new systems the resulting defence budget is still far greater than at any time since the

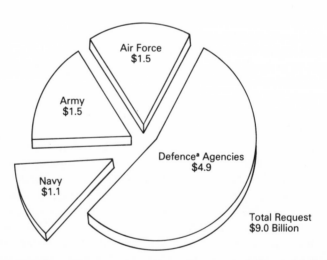

Figure 1 Fiscal 1985 Science and Technology Programme (billions of dollars)

ᵃ Includes Strategic Defense Initiative funding

Source: Report of the Secretary to the Congress, *FY1986 Budget, FY1987 Authorization Request and FY1986–1990 Defense Programs*, 4 February 1985, p. 264.

Vietnam conflict.[39] Much of the 1984 presidential campaign rhetoric centred on how to fund both security needs and social programmes given the announced objective of both parties to achieve a balanced budget. While Mr Reagan saw revenue enhancement in terms of the dynamics created by his 'supply-side' economics Mr Mondale, the Democratic contender, was more traditional in his call for an increase in revenue through higher taxes. The resilience of the American economy has allowed Mr Reagan the flexibility to implement his defence budget while still maintaining the highest deficit in American history in a domestic political atmosphere where debates over proposed cuts in social spending are yet unresolved. The legacy that Mr Reagan will apparently leave his successor are the fixed costs associated with these on-line weapons systems designed to project American power in keeping with his perception of the global threat emanating from the Soviet Union. Even if a new President desired to scale down the missions to be performed by American forces the amount available for social programmes would still be questionable since pressure would ensue to divert these savings toward long-range deficit reduction. The net effect is that social and security spending in the United States are not directly related, with the former assuming second place to military requirements and resources generated by an economy based on marked swings in productivity, inflation and output.

The situation in Western Europe is different and made even more complex by a combination of major social programmes, passive economies and different intraregional potentials and objectives. Three issues in particular serve to focus attention on these different patterns of perception between social and security spending held in the United States and in Western Europe. Foremost and central to the development of a post-war European economy was the increased role of government in the accumulation and distribution of available resources. Whether Marshall Plan funds or self-generated, government intervention and direction based on a loose but generally accepted socialist economic philosophy became the norm. The increased vitality of the post-war economy did not disrupt this pattern notwithstanding regular and often unplanned changes in government. Institutionalized through the French five-year plans or merely accepted as necessary by British Conservatives, demands on central resources continued as the needs of the population evolved from simple survival to a search for equality in opportunity and income. Programmes that in the United States would be viewed by neither party as within the purview of government were taken for granted in Europe at both citizen and governmental levels. Naturally the utilization of finite resources in

Table 2. Federal Budget Trends

Fiscal Year	Federal Outlays as % of GNP	DOD Outlays as a % of Federal Outlays	DOD Outlays as % of GNP	Non-DOD Outlays as % of Federal Outlays	Non-DOD Outlays as % of GNP	DOD Outlays as % of Net Public Spending*
1950	16.1	27.4	4.4	72.6	11.7	18.5
1955	18.0	51.3	9.2	48.7	8.8	35.5
1960	18.5	45.0	8.3	55.0	10.2	30.3
1965	18.0	38.7	7.0	61.3	11.0	25.2
1970	20.2	39.4	8.0	60.6	12.2	25.4
1971	20.4	35.4	7.2	64.6	13.2	22.4
1972	20.4	32.6	6.7	67.4	13.8	20.7
1973	19.6	29.8	5.8	70.2	13.8	19.0
1974	19.5	28.8	5.6	71.2	13.9	18.3
1975	22.5	25.5	5.7	74.5	16.7	16.5
1976	22.7	23.6	5.4	76.4	17.4	15.4
1977	22.0	23.4	5.1	76.6	16.8	15.5
1978	21.9	22.5	4.9	77.5	17.0	15.2
1979	21.4	22.8	4.9	77.2	16.5	15.4
1980	23.0	22.5	5.2	77.5	17.8	15.3
1981	23.5	23.0	5.4	77.0	18.1	15.8
1982	24.5	24.5	6.0	75.5	18.5	16.7
1983	25.1	25.4	6.4	74.6	18.7	17.4
1984	23.8	25.9	6.2	74.1	17.6	17.6
1985	24.8	25.7	6.4	74.3	18.4	17.5

* Federal, state and local net spending excluding government enterprises (such as the postal service and public utilities) except for any support these activities receive from tax funds.

Source: Report of the Secretary of Defense to the Congress, *FY1986 Budget, FY1987 Authorization Request and FY1986–1990 Defense Programs*, 4 February 1985, p, 295.

support of social programmes meant that funding for defence and security matters was moved to a secondary status. While standing forces and, for the UK and France, strategic assets, were accepted, overall military requirements and thus spending were limited and subordinated to the social agenda. This opportunity was made possible by the presence of American troops in Europe and the nuclear guarantees extended to the region by successive presidents. Within this security structure a tacit agreement for a 7:1 ratio of social to military spending was acknowledged as guiding European security outlays. The key to any increase rested in the revenue-producing qualities of European economies which in turn depended on their ability to compete against firms from the United States. The desire to enhance this competitive ability often necessitated government subsidies to firms which, when combined with the politically requisite need to maintain or increase social programmes, further diminished the funds available for defence and security matters. Dependence on American nuclear guarantees combined with static conventional forces ultimately allowed the Alliance military mission to be met by Europeans by defining it as regional and directed solely toward the Soviet threat. By so limiting the need for large military outlays the primacy of social spending in Europe was assured.

The second factor to influence perceptual differences between the United States and Western Europe has been the nature of their respective economic performances but especially when measured over the past ten years. While the monetary and economic disruptions in the aftermath of the 1974 oil crisis bedevilled both the American and European economies the short-term effect for both areas gave rise to distinctly different long-term compensating policies. The lack of government funds directly to offset the employment and production disruptions occasioned by the crisis meant an abrupt shift away from an American industrial base dependent on oil imports towards clean, high-technology, service-related firms. In contrast the decade of the 1970s found government subsidies in Europe being used to offset the higher prices and diminished market opportunities necessitated by the general disruptions in the global patterns of trade. In social terms the support policies of the Europeans contrasted favourably with lines of unemployed steel and automobile workers in the United States, but in reality served only to delay and increase the ultimate costs associated with future adjustments. By the early 1980s the American economy was productive and dynamic while European output lagged far behind. Inefficiencies created mainly by the more benign social outlook of European governments had created structural inequities in their capacity for international trade that had to be overcome by the introduction of measures which if not alien then certainly were not the norm within the European tradition.

Adding to the troubles associated with the need to restructure European industrial systems was the strength of the American dollar in global markets. Doubling in value against weak currencies such as the Italian lira, the dollar also moved up sharply against the base European currencies—the franc, the mark and the pound. Normally this change would provide the opportunity to increase European exports and thus offset the decrease in currency value. But the structural inefficiencies present in most European industrial sectors and to a certain extent the nationalization activities of the late 1970s combined to ensure that private capital available to prime an economic recovery was being diverted to high interest bearing accounts available only in the United States. Lacking these resources, European firms were hard pressed to introduce changes to enable their industrial output to sell in international competition. The 7:1 ratio of social to defence spending widened further as available resources were diverted to support social and industrial restructuring activities. As a result Europeans were unable to acquiesce to American demands that their NATO contributions increase by 3 per cent, further intertwining commercial conflict with security-related matters.[40]

Finally, and to add to the perceptual issues separating the United States and Western Europe, were those problems generated by intra-regional disparities in ability to adjust to these economically derived problems. Economically the members of the Community may be disposed into three separate levels with varying ability to adjust to externally derived challenges. The Northern tier including the UK, France and West Germany; the central group of Benelux, Denmark and Italy; and the poorer states of Ireland, Greece, Spain and Portugal. While enjoying equal membership in the Community their ability to adjust and minimize the effects of these economic challenges differs greatly. Without becoming lost in details it is really only the first group that has the flexibility, based on resources, market position and perhaps tradition, to weather and overcome these economic events with minimal external assistance. The second group has the ability to implement to varying degree measures that are the result of action taken in concert with others, in particular the first group of European states. The last group is generally in a position to react to problems with little clear ability to influence the direction of a solution. Indeed a major stimulus to Community membership for this latter group was the desire to minimize internal economic disruptions by tying their economies to those of the first two groups of states. A by-product of these issues has been the less than overwhelming support by the first group to additional members given the increased drain on resources presented by these newcomers. These disparities have given strength to the pursuit of a 'two-speed' Europe where states catch up to regional initiatives when their assets and outlooks allow such progress.[41]

The net result of these factors is that the relationship of social to defence spending is viewed differently in Europe than in the United States. Resource availability, public inputs and government–firm relations suggest a lesser ability for European governments to increase defence spending even if agreement is reached at official levels. The defeat of the British Labour Party in 1983 essentially because of their semi-pacifist platform has not been translatable by the victorious Conservative Party into support for a build-up of military forces. The sentiment in European public circles appears to centre on maintaining sufficiency of defence needs but not at the expense of social programmes. Sufficiency is nationally derived and somewhat inchoate in nature but one can suggest that the ability of European states to meet that objective will not increase in the future. Thus unilateral security-directed programmes must gradually give way toward greater co-operative action. The ability of European NATO governments to structure that cooperative response will therefore depend greatly on the level and nature of public opinion on the topic and salience of harmonizing European security policy.

PUBLIC OPINION AND THE EVOLUTION OF EUROPEAN SECURITY POLICY

Although essential, the relationship of public opinion to the process of security planning in democratic societies is often difficult to assess. Even when available, survey data is often nationally bound and difficult to compare across borders. When cross-national data does exist it is too often tied to specific events in a manner that makes its long-term predictive value uncertain. This is particularly true for issues of national security which address the sensational event often to the exclusion of underlying policy. Public support for the general concepts of deterrence coexist with a desire to diminish defence spending in a fashion that tends to neutralize the usefulness of survey results. Mass demonstrations reflect key issues but how deeply and by what propor-tion of the society remain unclear. What role do public outpourings of sentiment on INF have on government decision processes? None the less, the long-term stability of democratic societies depends on the acceptance of the need for security expenditures by the public or at least the neglect of the issue by its more vocal members. Thus public opinion data must at least be weighed even if later discounted by the decision-makers.

The salience of the issue of Western security requirements and defence postures prompted the 1985 release of a major cross-national survey designed to assess relatively equivalent questions among NATO publics.[42] While not perfect in its dimensions or methodology, the survey does allow more than conjecture in attempting to assess the role of publics in the current debate over NATO and the European concern for its security future. This data will be arrayed in response to five key questions:

1. What is the perception held of the role of the United States in European defence matters?
2. How is the Soviet Union's military presence viewed by European NATO citizens?
3. What is NATO's future role, including the possibility of a greater European component within or alongside the present structure?
4. How deep and how widespread is the level of European support for the issues of neutrality or peace?
5. Is there a gap between elite and mass sentiment on the issue of European security and, if so, what role does the public play in any decisions?

Although the data is heavily weighted toward the four major European states—France, Italy, West Germany and the United Kingdom— smaller states, in particular the Netherlands, are also included in the results.

Perceptions of the American role in European security

Clearly the United States and its foreign policy remain focal points for European public opinion. Just as certainly perceptions of the American role in global affairs have changed in the past decade. Three dimensions of the American role in European security matters emerge from the data. The first concerns the general attitude held toward the United States by European publics. Confidence in the United States as a traditional ally and friend remains high, reaching 70 per cent in the UK and varying between 50 per cent and 65 per cent in the other states surveyed.[43] This measure of support though quickly erodes when the specific issues of the American ability to handle world problems is queried. In 1978, 71 per cent of Italians responded affirmatively to this question, a figure which dropped to 55 per cent in 1982. United Kingdom figures were even more dramatic with 60 per cent responding 'not at all confident' in February 1982.[44] In the Netherlands the survey sought to elicit anti-American feelings and found 47 per cent negative or very negative toward the United States essentially because of Reagan administration policies and the INF deployment decision.[45]

The second dimension that emerges concerns the perceived threat posed by the United States toward Europe. A surprising number, 35 per cent in the United Kingdom, saw the United States as a military threat or, as in Italy, felt that American policies were likely to promote the chance of war (44 per cent).[46] While the military dimension of this threat is very real, it is the economic aspect that ultimately emerges as the central concern. Consistently respondents felt that the most important aspect of American–European relations was economic in nature.[47] The French response, where 43 per cent were more afraid of American monetary policy than Soviet defence policy, while not typical in its wording, was characteristic of the level of feeling on this issue.[48]

The final dimension, and one that inferentially combines the previous two, concerns the direction of American–European relations. Here the data are clear in their conclusion that relations are moving apart at a fairly dramatic rate. In the UK and West Germany, two states with especially close ties to the United States, the figures are particularly revealing (see Table 3). This general sentiment toward the American government was best summed up in the French survey results which assessed the relationship with the United States as

Table 3. Anglo–American and German–American Relations

Closeness of Relations between Britain and the United States			
	4/82	6/82	11/82
Drawing closer	42%	50%	20%
No change	19	21	19
Further apart	31	23	53

Source: Gallup June 1982.

'In what direction have relations between FRG and US changed since Reagan took office?'

	8/81	5/82
Better	9%	5%
Same	49	51
Worse	42	43

Source: Hans Rattinger, 'The Federal Republic of Germany,' in, *The Public and Atlantic Defense*, p. 140.

containing 'moments of irritation against a background of general skepticism toward the ally on the other side of the Atlantic'.[49]

The nature of the threat posed by the Soviet Union

The generally negative impression of the Soviet Union held by most Western Europeans since the end of World War Two continues to predominate. Even among French Communist Party members, traditional supporters of Soviet policies, there has been a noticeable shift in willingness to criticize political conditions in the Soviet Union.[50] Although Europeans remain critical of current Soviet policies there has also been a shift in the nature of the threat felt to be posed by that state. While 66 per cent of West German respondents held the Soviet Union to be a threat in 1952, only 44 per cent agreed with that assessment in 1983. In that same survey 15 per cent held the Soviet Union to be no threat in 1952, while 49 per cent held that same view in 1983.[51]

This change in attitude may be partially explained by data which suggest that Soviet aims are perceived as designed to achieve military superiority over the United States and not designed to attack or even threaten Western Europe.[52] Consistently respondents rated the East superior now and in the future in military terms, perhaps explaining an apparent desire to play down the threat posed by a decidedly stronger adversary. Consistent with this sentiment there appears an increased willingness to portray the reasons for existing global tensions in East–West terms, thus again shifting the burden for resolution to both superpowers and further insulating Europe from the need to choose sides in the debate.[53]

The future of NATO and the issue of increased European responsibility for its own security requirements

While support for NATO remains high among respondents, their answers on three issues integral to that organization's continued integrity yield somewhat contradictory results. Although public ignorance on defence specifics questions the reliability of data and indirectly the ability to treat NATO and derivitive issues as a coherent whole, there is no question but that public sentiment is supportive, however unknowingly, of changes in the American–European military alliance.

Intermediate-range Nuclear Force (INF) deployments

The 1979 NATO 'twin-track' decision engendered open protests in Western Europe and led to a reappraisal of the role of the United

States and nuclear weapons for European security. Although government support for the deployment decision, even in non-participatory France, was consistently strong, public reaction was decidedly less supportive.

In West Germany only 35 per cent of citizens favoured the INF decision.[54] In a parallel survey 63 per cent favoured the Soviet call for a moratorium on all deployments even though the status quo would work to the distinct disadvantage of NATO. Similar figures exist for Italy with 40 per cent opposed to deployment, a number jumping to 50 per cent after the decision to base Cruise missiles in Comiso, Sicily, was actually taken. Parallel figures emerge for all surveyed states.[55] Although opposition tends to strengthen the further left one moves on the political spectrum, the data suggest that negative views on INF are spread, albeit unevenly, across the ideological board.

The role and level of defence spending

The current official desire to minimize the role of nuclear weapons in Europe, perhaps through an enhanced conventional capability, does not translate into public support for the need dramatically to increase defence spending to fund such a change. Several possible explanations, including a desire for no nuclear weapons or ignorance of the cost of conventional alternatives, might be suggested. Clearly there is major support, reaching as high as 80 per cent in the Netherlands, to decrease defence costs, often accompanied by a desire to redirect savings to enhance social spending.[56]

The sluggishness and unemployment level of Western European economies over the past few years has underscored the need to, at minimum, continue the present levels of socially directed spending. The question becomes how to sustain those guarantees without also restructuring the industrial base that is ultimately responsible for the revenue to continue such supports. In the short term one can revitalize national industries and global competitive capability, or instead cut other programmes to redirect finite resources to the social sector. While the Thatcher concept of 'privatization' is an example of the former option, most European governments continue to practice the politics of redistribution, slighting non-social-programme sectors and hoping to recoup losses when the economy enters an upswing. Both options though assume the primacy of domestic economic objectives, relegate defence spending to a secondary role and further blur the clarity of the debate over conventional versus nuclear deterrence for Europe's security future.

A new European role in security policy

Spirited public opposition to INF and a demonstrated aversion to increased defence spending suggests an opportunity for a new security policy thrust in Europe. Although the failure of the EDC and the multilateral force (MLF) in previous decades muted the calls for an increased European role for its security, current demonstrations favouring a decrease in defence outlays and lessened American dominance again raise the salience of this issue. When coupled with the environmental changes effected by the general global decline in American leadership the opportunity for a new European effort designed to re-establish a major role in security and defence matters emerges.

The data provide a good opportunity to discuss public opinion on the general issue of NATO and the specific question of an increased European role in security policy (see Table 4). When interpreting these data one must never lose sight of the fact that while most respondents have heard of NATO less than one-third know what the acronym and inferentially what the institution stands for.[57] Not surprisingly support for the status quo, in this instance remaining in NATO, heads the list of choices. But, more importantly, support for either an increased European role in NATO or sympathy for a completely separate European defence entity is quite strong. This strength is even more impressive given the minimal attention previously afforded this option by government officials or the media. Now that the topic has become more public in its presentation it remains an open question if this level of support will be sustained in pursuit of coordinated European security policy options in the near future.

Table 4. Public opinion on NATO and Europe's security-policy role (per cent)

	United Kingdom 2/82	France 2/80	Italy 3/81	Netherlands 3/81
Stay in NATO	37	–	30	31
Stay in with unified European command	20	23	25	15
Independent European command not allied to the United States	10	28	15	11

Source: Gregory Flynn and Hans Rattinger, eds, *The Public and Atlantic Defense*, 1985.

The appeal of neutralism and pacificism

The issues of pacificism, neutralism, decreased defence spending and the role of NATO are intertwined to an extent that makes disaggregation of responses difficult and long-term trend prediction somewhat speculative. Although data and questions on these issues are not easily comparable the cross nationally of two of the surveys, on sympathy for peace demonstrations (Table 5) and on attitudes towards neutralism

Table 5. Sympathy for European peace demonstrations, November 1981 (per cent)

	Netherlands	France	United Kingdom	West Germany
Totally agree	46%	22%	23%	23%
Mostly agree	33	28	29	36
Mostly disagree	9	13	15	22
Totally disagree	8	21	24	16
No answer/don't know	4	16	9	3

Source: Gregory Flynn and Hans Rattinger, eds, *The Public and Atlantic Defense*, 1985.

(Table 6), does allow at least preliminary assessments to be advanced. While sympathy for peace demonstrations appears widespread there are distinct national differences on what constituted 'sympathy'. In West Germany respondents were asked in June 1983: 'What actions would you take if new missiles were to be deployed where you live?' The results are given below:

Petition	60%
Demonstrate	28%
Blockade installations	7%
Illegal demonstrations	6%
Damage installations	1%

In comparison French and Italian respondents overwhelmingly viewed demonstrations as something essentially foreign in nature, limiting their own roles to passive support of an external phenomenon rather than as a viable option for use in their own domestic political debates.[58] Clearly the publics of three states, the United Kingdom, West Germany and the Netherlands, have an active sense of what demonstrations accomplish, while Italy and France appear more passive in their views. Naturally the actual deployment of missiles in the first group, coupled with their sense of being major targets in any conflict, account for their more vocal sense of opposition. The inclusion of Italy

Table 6. Sympathy for a move towards neutralism
in the East–West Conflict (per cent)

	Yes	No	No answer/don't know
Holland	53	32	15
France	43	41	16
UK	45	48	13
West Germany	57	43	–
United States	41	45	14

Source: Newsweek, 31 January 1983.

in the second group is perhaps best explained by the traditional North–South division in that country. Placement of the missiles in the South was politically popular because of the rural, politically under-developed and economically depressed nature of that area. Demonstrations in the more radical enclaves of Bologna and Milan in the North failed to transmit their enthusiasm to the South and, in so failing, isolated the demonstrators from the physical objects of their scorn. As one analyst suggested the failure of the Italian movement to reach 'critical mass' was due to two factors: firstly, the perception that the anti-nuclear movement had foreign roots; and secondly, that the movement is perceived by the majority of voters as being controlled by radical political elements.[59]

   In France the lack of anti-nuclear sentiment is consistent with general sympathy for an independent foreign policy based on the possession of nuclear weapons. This support is shared by a majority of even the French Communist Party, thus sheltering the government from demonstrations and similar actions.[60]

Elite and public perceptions on European security policy

The NATO 'twin-track' decision engendered a major outpouring of anti-nuclear, pro-peace rallies in Western Europe especially in the crucial pre-deployment phase of the autumn of 1983. Massive street demonstrations and sit-ins at places such as Greenham Common sought to underscore dramatically the need to actively oppose the East–West arms spiral. Notwithstanding effects on the Eurostrategic balance, Cruise and Pershing IIs became the symbol of American military aggressiveness and European impotence to stand against the will of the dominant Alliance partner. Although opposition changed after deployment into channels as diverse as new political groups or overt action or terrorism against missile sites and military personnel, the question remains as to the depth of sentiment represented by this movement and its ability to effect change at governmental level on the issues of further deployments and security consensus in Western Europe.

Survey data on this question tend to suggest that, while demonstrations were reflective of intensely held feelings, that sentiment has once again been submerged to a secondary position behind more prosaic but ultimately more personally relevant concerns such as income and jobs. This sublimation has been assisted by tacit party agreements, especially in Italy, to keep defence and foreign policy issues in the background so as not to confuse an electorate already overwhelmed by domestic political concerns.[61] Even the British Labour Party, after suffering its worst defeat since 1918, has toned down its anti-NATO stance in pursuit of voter support in future national elections.

The diminishing hold on the public's attention generated by peace issues has been assisted by the Western European tendency to insulate foreign policy, including defence and security matters, from direct public participation. Involvement of the public in such matters was characterized by one West German author as 'unpredictable, paradoxical and inconsistent', underscoring the general lack of public interest and indeed knowledge required to maintain the level of enthusiasm requisite to an effective pro-peace movement.[62] With the exception of small radical groups, which pride themselves on being intellectual leaders on the arcana of deterrence theory, even antideployment parties such as the West German SPD have returned to the mainstream issues of inflation and employment. In one way, though, the pro-peace movement does line up with current more deeply held, and thus probably more central, voter concerns. That overlap is in the area of defence spending. Overwhelmingly respondents sought to cut national defence budgets principally by eliminating future big ticket items. Thus while 79 per cent of British women opposed the Labour Party's call to scrap the Poseidon submarine force, 50 per cent were opposed to its replacement by the Trident system.[63] In a similar fashion, although 53 per cent of French respondents agreed that spending on military research and development was necessary to 'technological innovation and economic growth', 40 per cent felt that further planned development of the French nuclear arsenal was a waste of scarce resources.[64]

One final factor concerning the ability of such pro-peace sentiment to affect national policy must be addressed. Consistently three distinct sometimes overlapping groups were represented in peace demonstrations: women, youth and fringe political or ideological parties and groups. The data strongly suggest that the views of these groups are more pro-peace than those of the population as a whole. Although these groups represent a sizable proportion of the European population they do not hold a commensurate position in the policy-making or even policy-affecting sectors. In effect their positions are not easily translated into policy initiatives since they are often viewed as inconsistent with sentiments held in more traditional power centres. This ineffectualness is further diluted by their tendency to vote based on more traditional factors such as class or religion than on the ideological stances of peace and neutralism. ·

This chapter has traced the evolution of the myriad of issues now current in American–European relations. Additionally it has sought to raise the role of the Community in the possible resolution or at least the management of those interactions. This study now turns to an analysis of how the Community has previously sought to deal with many of these externally generated problems while simultaneously pursuing the internal objectives directed by the tenets of integration.

NOTES

1. U.S. Arms Control and Disarmament Agency, *Commentary on SALT I and SALT II: Texts and Histories*, 1980.
2. *NATO Today: The Alliance in Evolution*, Report to the Committee on Foreign Relations, US Senate, April 1982, Chapter 5.
3. William Mako, *U.S. Ground Forces and the Defense of Central Europe* (Washington, DC: The Brookings Institute, 1983), p. 8.
4. John Lewis Gaddis, 'Containment: Its Past and Future', *International Security*, 5, 4 (Spring 1981), pp. 74–102.
5. *NATO Today: The Alliance in Evolution*, Chapter 1.
6. Mako, *U.S. Ground Forces and the Defense of Central Europe*, pp. 23–5.
7. H. J. Neuman, *Nuclear Forces in Europe* (London: IISS, 1982), p. 6.
8. Jeffrey Richelson, 'PD-59, NSDD-13 and the Reagan Strategic Modernization Program', *The Journal of Strategic Studies*, 6, 2 (June 1983), pp. 125–46.
9. Neuman, op. cit.
10. Colin Gray, 'What Deters? The Ability to Wage Nuclear War', *International Security*, 4, 1 (Summer 1979), pp. 54–87.
11. Henry Kissinger, 'A Plan to Re-shape NATO', *Time*, 5 March 1984; and a response by Alois Mertes, 'What Should be done to change NATO', *The German Tribune: Political Affairs Review*, no. 48, 1 July 1984, pp. 1–5.
12. 'NATO Trying to Answer U.S. Critics on Spending', *International Herald Tribune*, 14 November 1984, p. 1.
13. Werner Kaltefleiter, *The Strategic Defense Initiative: Some Implications for Europe* (London: Institute for European Defence and Strategic Studies, occasional paper 10, February 1985).

14. Stanley Hoffmann, 'Gaullism by Any Other Name', *Foreign Policy*, 57 (Winter 1984–5), pp. 38–57.
15. 'Mitterrand Said to Fear Brain Drain and Unrest', *New York Times*, 7 May 1985, p. 1.
16. European Parliament Working Document, *Motion for a Resolution on the Two-part NATO Decision*, September 1981, Doc. 1-497/81, PE 74.787; Wolfgang Kist, 'Europe Etats-Unis: le malaise', *30 Jours d'Europe*, 314–5 (September–October 1984), pp. 7–10.
17. Leslie Gelb, 'Is the Nuclear Threat Manageable?', *New York Times Magazine*, 4 March 1984.
18. 'Aide Says Kohl Wants to Avoid Bonn Debate on "Star Wars" Role', *New York Times*, 3 September 1985, p. 4; 'Thatcher, Her Party in a Slump, Shakes up Cabinet', *New York Times*, 3 September 1985, p. 3.
19. David Greenwood, 'Strengthening Conventional Deterrence', *NATO Review*, 4 (August 1984), pp. 8–12.
20. General Bernard Rogers, 'Follow-on Forces Attack (FOFA): Myths and Realities', *NATO Review*, 6 (December 1984), pp. 1–9; Christopher Donnelly, 'The Development of the Soviet Concept of Echeloning', *NATO Review*, 6 (December 1984), pp. 9–17.
21. European Parliament Working Document, *Report on European Political Cooperation and European Security*, 3 December 1982, Doc. 1-946/82, PE 80.082.
22. 'When Pinch Comes to Squeeze', *The Economist*, 10 August 1985, pp. 35–6.
23. *NATO Today: The Alliance in Evolution*, Chapter 5.
24. Gaddis, 'Containment: Its Past and Future'.
25. See the earlier discussion on vulnerability and sensitivity dependence.
26. Christopher Hill, ed., *National Foreign Policies and European Political Cooperation* (London: George Allen & Unwin, 1983).
27. J.-J. Servan-Schreiber, *The American Challenge* (New York: Avon Books, 1967).
28. Raymond Vernon, *Big Business and the State—Changing Relations in Western Europe* (London: Macmillan Press, 1974), p. 11.
29. Christopher Layton, *Cross Frontier Mergers in Europe—How Can Government Help?* (Bath: Bath University Press, 1971).
30. EC Commission, *The Community's Industrial Policy*, 18 March 1970 (Brussels: EC Bulletin Supplement 4/1970).
31. Anne Daltrop, *Politics and the European Community* (Harlow: Longman Group Ltd, 1982), pp. 138–42.
32. Benjamin Cohen, 'Europe's Money, America's Problem', *Foreign Policy*, 35 (Summer 1979), pp. 31–48.
33. EC Commission, *The Development Cooperation Policies of the European Community*, April 1977.
34. John Van Oudenaren, *The Urengoi Pipeline: Prospects for Soviet Leverage* (Santa Monica, CA: Rand Corporation, 1984).
35. Jonathan Stern, 'Spectre and Pipe Dreams', *Foreign Policy*, 1982.
36. 'U.S. Technology Transfer Practices Will Guide European Reaction to SDI', *Aviation Week and Space Technology*, 3 June 1985, p. 125.
37. Gaddis, 'Containment: Its Past and Future'.
38. Barry Posen and Stephen Van Evera, 'Defense Policy and the Reagan Administration: Departure from Containment', *International Security*, 7, 1 (Summer 1983), pp. 3–45.
39. *U.S. Defense Policy*, 3rd edn (Washington, DC: Congressional Quarterly, Inc., 1983), p. 9.

40. *NATO Today: The Alliance in Evolution*.
41. 'One and Two Don't Make Three', *The Economist*, 9 March 1985, p. 50.
42. Gregory Flynn and Hans Rattinger, eds, *The Public and Atlantic Defense* (London: Croom Helm, 1985).
43. Ibid., p. 40.
44. ibid., p. 197.
45. Ibid., p. 41.
46. Ibid., pp. 19, 198.
47. Ibid., p. 139.
48. Ibid., pp. 19, 91, 139.
49. Ibid., p. 89.
50. Ibid., p. 71.
51. Ibid., p. 118.
52. Ibid., p. 183.
53. Ibid., p. 228.
54. Ibid., p. 134.
55. Ibid., pp. 191–2.
56. Ibid., pp. 188, 235.
57. Ibid., p. 44.
58. Ibid., pp. 82, 175.
59. Ibid., p. 175.
60. Ibid., p. 83.
61. Ibid., p. 177.
62. Ibid., p. 100.
63. Ibid., p. 49.
64. Ibid., p. 80.

3 The legacy of Community failures in high technology

The two previous chapters detailed the evolving international economic and security environment and the need for a regional response to change, but left unanswered what part the Community has played in those interactions in the past. While the defence aspects of American–European interactions have recently become visible, the underlying economic aspects of that dyadic relationship have been the topic of long-standing and vocal debate. To define current Community policies and options without acknowledging those previous programmes would be a disservice. Given the central importance of high-technology industries to the overarching issues of economic and security competition, analysis must of necessity focus on these concerns. But to concentrate on the entire Community programme in the area of economics would be to distort its value for the question of an evolving security policy. In order not to trivialize through generalization, this chapter will focus on the Community's efforts to address the external competition generated by primarily American multinational enterprises (MNEs). The issue of MNEs is not merely economic in scope but also involves political and defence matters. The use of the MNE for analysis also directly relates to the development of a Community security policy in several ways. In the first place, MNEs have the major role in the industrial production of high-technology goods with their dual civilian and military applications. Second, MNEs active in the security sector are generally of two types—either American subsidiaries or wholly owned by European states. Their corporate activities are thus a microcosm of the larger American–Community economic rivalry. Third, much of the Community's internal movement toward economic and industrial union has been generated as a response to the competitive threat posed by these external transnational actors. Internal progress has been delineated as a response to external threats in the past and provides a firm basis for the inference that the changing security environment will require compensating internal adjustment in the future. Finally, MNEs and their control over the factors of production that are essential to Community employment and quality of life suggests the need to assess from a broad perspective the regional role of these foreign actors.

TECHNOLOGY PRODUCTION AND USE: THE ROLE OF FOREIGN
COMPANIES IN THE COMMUNITY

Common Market to Paris Summit: 1958–72

Western Europe has perennially been a net importer of raw materials which are then processed and exported in finished form often back to the extractive supplier. Much of the colonial history of Europe was denominated as a search for both materials and markets.[1] The price differential between raw and finished goods, coupled with the trade stability inherent in colonial or commonwealth relations, ensured a favourable balance of payments for Europe. Based upon this industrial prowess European revenue and economic stature were ensured by the value added to raw materials in pursuit of foreign market opportunities. Direct foreign investment in exploitive industries, such as mining, was generally concentrated in former colonial territories and was designed to provide the raw materials required for the finishing process in European factories. An alternative type of investment, portfolio or indirect in nature, was concentrated in markets such as the American where the European objective was a return on capital rather than operational control of the foreign venture.[2] Intra-European patterns of corporate growth were based on these international relationships and market patterns. In contrast European markets were viewed in primarily national terms which sought to develop and secure an oligopolistic position in a product and then selectively to export that product to the rest of Europe protected by private reciprocal agreements and cartel arrangements.[3] When a decision was made to expand across national borders such activity tended to occur in contiguous European states and in particular in countries sharing similar cultural, linguistic and ethnic qualities.

Business competition for the European firm had therefore long since ceased to be a major operational factor. Cartel arrangements, external investments and delineated sales areas effectively served to apportion markets among national firms. This arrangement resulted in a European market area of small firms each producing a single line of goods with annual returns based on these fixed price agreements rather than on competition between different products. The net result was a static market with no incentive and indeed little capital available to improve on product diversity, quality or innovation.

This corporate complaisance was quickly dismantled with the establishment of the Common Market when American firms with their diverse product lines, long production runs and competitive instincts set out to capture significant portions of this new market area. This challenge to the European firm was intensified by the American MNEs' ability successfully to exploit the existing economic system of international trade in its favour. Their operational style of corporate control through direct investment, professional management and market control through product innovation was a result of the American anti-trust system which disallowed the cartellization practised in Europe. In Servan-Schreiber's terms, 'American MNE success resulted from the extension to Europe of an art of organization that is still a mystery to us'.[4] The initial European response was to adopt and adapt the organizational techniques championed by these American competitors to their own market requirements. Industrial cooperation between European firms was viewed as essential to survival. In particular business training for managers, increased firm mergers and pooling of research and development assets were proposed to restructure staid and tradition-bound European firms into internationally competitive entities.

Although this response was economic and industrial in form it paralleled the efforts toward political integration then being pursued within the Community. Indeed this period of industrial activity, 1958–72, precisely overlaps the greatest sense of movement toward political community. From the completion of the customs union, earlier than planned, in 1968 to the positive declarations of political unity voiced after the 1969 and 1972 European summits a single Community appeared closer than at any time since the inception of the Market in 1958. Given this overlap the desire to reorganize European firms was considered to be the result of these integrative efforts rather than a response to the dominant competitive rationale of the American MNE operating model. As Raymond Vernon noted: 'If the EC grows larger and more cohesive . . . there will be a growing tendency for larger European owned enterprises inside the area to think of their market as pan-European rather than national'.[5]

The immediate objective for European firms was to attain the benefits of economy of scale that had served the American MNE so well over time. Europeans were quick to recognize those benefits given the visible market-place now controlled by a small number of American firms surrounded by a fragmented sea of small European companies. Where the vertical integration of IBM allowed it to develop, manufacture and market computers within one structure, similar operations were performed in Europe by numerous and small-scale firms. This nascent European response was also being channelled to pursue an international competitive position by adapting 'industrial structures to the technological needs of the second half of the 20th century'.[6] A symbiotic relationship between international competitive capability and the objectives of European integration was now complete and was to be pursued by regional planning measures.

Progress towards the goals of political union and global economic prowess were now increasingly being identified as outcomes of those externally derived competitive pressures. The long-term European response was now to be delineated through sustained efforts by governments to encourage firm mergers, particularly within the high-technology sectors. This included the creation of what has been termed the 'national champion', an enterprise responsive to its government's needs and entitled to its preferential support. From the outset government support for these mergers was strong and much of this industrial restructuring was under the direct control of national holding companies such as the Industrial Reorganization Corporation (IRC) in the UK, the Institute for Industrial Reconstruction (IRI) in Italy or through the *indicatif* of the French five-year plan.[7] By 1971 the number of European firms independently active in the high-technology fields had been substantially reduced and subjected in large measure to varying but high levels of government control.

In addition to the creation of national champions were measures to promote joint research and development resource allocation between national firms. Since such cooperation did not involve the loss of corporate identity or national revenue it was favourably viewed by relevant governments and supervisory bureaucracies. The primary objective of coordinating European research and development resources was to counter the massive subsidies provided to high-technology firms by the American government through its provision of public contracts, defence spending and the import barriers of the Buy American Act. In contrast industrial fragmentation in Europe had resulted in small amounts of available capital to support firms where research rather than raw materials was the key to success: 'A ... main factor behind the Agfa-Gevaert merger was the fact that Gevaert's total sales were only just about equivalent to the amount spent by Kodak on research alone'.[8] Pooling of research and development moneys was especially important in those advanced technology areas where start-up costs and the need continually to upgrade processes required capital, personnel and other resources in short supply throughout Europe.

To complement these national efforts government policy statements now began to stress the necessity for European rather than strictly national criteria when pursuing programmes in crucial industrial sectors.[9] Business groups as a rule were willing to endorse these regional efforts in order to capture larger international market sectors for their products. Slogans such as 'National independence is national impotence', summed up the feeling that Community solutions were the key to meeting foreign competition. There was little effort made to disengage the process of internally directed regional integration from the demands imposed by the external competition of the foreign firm. To complete the political community would, by definition, solve the competitive challenge posed by the American firm. European integration could only be enhanced by national mergers and the pooling and joint utilization of research and development resources. The fact that American firms had already penetrated the European market to such an extent that they often proved to be better partners for expansion plans than were Community firms was often overlooked in the desire to equate intra-market industrial cooperation with a heightened sense of the pace of integration. Although this misperception was caused by the overlap of two distinct developmental processes, that of regional integration and that of international economic interdependence, it was only in the aftermath of the 1973 oil crisis that the differences between each process become apparent.[10]

OPEC to Fontainebleau: 1973–84

The OPEC-inspired oil crisis effectively brought to an end the movement toward internally driven regional integration as Community members scrambled to secure their supplies with little reference to or concern about coordinated policy responses. Even if it had not been the oil crisis then some other event would have precipitated the unravelling of internally derived regional integration efforts. For what drove the re-emergence of national plans to the exclusion of regional initiatives was the change in the sustaining international economic system. A dismantling of the dollar as the global reserve currency joined with domestic industrial cutbacks in the United States to point out the fragility of a global system buoyed by only one state. The aura of the American MNE was tarnished as even major firms such as Chrysler had first to sell their overseas assets and then to petition for government assistance. The cutback in NASA funding had served to minimize the use of American government contracts as a source of technological spin-offs applicable to more marketable civilian applications. The ability of both Japan and OPEC to challenge American industrial dominance merely underscored that realignment not only in the factors of production but also in the centres of responsibility. To suggest that the not yet completed Community push for a regional response could outweigh a desire for national control even at the expense of international competitiveness would be to place the ideal above the reality.

The oil crisis thus served to make explicit the fact that most of the internal realignment of Community industries in the previous decade was a response to externally generated competitive elements, rather than an outgrowth of an orderly march toward integration. National programmes now reassumed the initiative as regional resources and will proved insufficient to the task. The development of national champions provided states with ready-made vehicles by which to direct their assets in pursuit of decidedly national objectives. Although cooperative research and development and marketing schemes did persist they were more likely to fail given the desire of each state to maintain control over money, personnel and application of any consortium effort. This was the fate of the Unidata computer group formed by France, the Netherlands and West Germany in 1973 and dismantled in 1975.[11] A few commercial projects such as Airbus were able to overcome this trend but only at the cost of massive state financial support and changes in the international trading environment that were not to become apparent for many years. Greater success was evinced in military ventures such as the Tornado but the benefits of this cooperation, because of its defence orientation, were kept separate from any commercial spin-offs for Community utilization.

Regional programmes to continue the drive towards the development of large-scale industries with the financial, personnel and coordination resources essential to international competitiveness also floundered. Two specific proposals are indicative of the innovative efforts devised by the Community during this period and the difficulty or impossibility of implementing change in the face of a return to national direction of business assets. Recognizing the major role played in the high-technology area by state public contracts, the Community sought to create a regional market for such opportunities. While general public contracts accounted for 5–9 per cent of gross internal product, those in the advanced technology and allied sectors accounted for 30–40 per cent of all such contracts within the Community area.[12] The Community's proposal would require all public contracts to be let at a particular time and place with bids from throughout the region being offered at that instance. Competition between similar nationally sponsored projects would be minimized since coordination of programmes would take place prior to the bidding process. The Commission stated that their objective was 'the effective establishment of a single market in technologically advanced products for the Community as a whole'.[13] Although finally passed in 1976, the effective implementation of this proposal continues to be a major source of concern.[14] The second proposal was the attempt to introduce the Community Development Contract (CDC) to assist the advanced technology sectors of the economy.[15] By substituting Community financing for national assistance the Commission sought to unify capability then blocked by the concept of 'fair return' on investment. These contracts were to be offered to consortia of European firms which sought to increase their competitive capability in the advanced technology sectors of the global market. This proposal was one of several, including the European Export Bank (EEB), designed to promote the completion of the internal market by allowing coordinated efforts to have a chance of success against foreign competition.[16] Although strongly supported by the affected industries the reluctance of members to cede any control over these sectors allowed these proposals to wither from neglect until formally withdrawn in 1980.

In addition to creating the ability to coordinate capability through procurement and the opportunity to self-finance through CDCs and the EEB, the Community introduced more comprehensive proposals to channel the development of the entire sector of Community firms active in advanced technology areas.[17] The 1970 industrial policy had differentiated between two types of industries that required regional assistance if they were to respond to externally generated economic challenges. The first were those industries such as textiles and steel that were losing market shares to the less costly environments of states such as Taiwan. Here the Community's proposal was to rationalize production capability within the Market in order gradually to limit the persons and firms active in this sector. The recognition was that the Community as a whole should gradually phase out of or at least minimize its role in sectors where they could no longer hope to compete with Third World producers. The use of the Community Social Fund to assist in the retraining of displaced workers would assist national programmes during this transition.

The second category of industry identified for assistance by the industrial policy were those in the growth sectors, whose viability in global competition was integral to Community plans. Industries such as aerospace, data processing and innovations research were identified as those areas where the Community sought to develop and sustain an international capability geared towards regional as well as foreign markets. These industries had not benefited greatly from the completion of the internal market since their opportunities were still bounded by 'the cages formed by the structures of each state'.[18] The requirements of this sector included sophisticated research capabilities, high levels of available capital and skilled labour and were felt to mirror the Community's vision of where Europe should fit in in the coming decades. Unlike the first category, the Community envisaged assuming direct control of these sectors and, by so minimizing national roles, better rationalizing and directing a regional response. Although far-sighted and responsive to economically dictated conditions, these proposals were out of touch with the return to national control which occurred in the aftermath of the oil crisis. While never fully implemented the original and follow-on proposals for these growth sectors are still important to underscore errors and suggest remaining policy threads that have re-emerged to form the basis of current initiatives in these areas. Two specific aspects of the 1970 industrial policy, informatics and aerospace, merit particular attention.

The Community and the informatics industry

Although denominated as an integral part of the Community's internally driven economic and industrial programmes, progress in informatics was actually a response to the competition generated by one foreign firm, IBM. IBM's ability to self-finance innovations and then market them through its captive system of customers had enabled it to not only dominate the global market but also to set the standards to which its competitors had to adapt (see Table 7). To compete, European companies had several options: 'go-it-alone' national programmes, European cooperation or European–American arrangements. In addition, European firms had to decide whether to compete across the board or to select certain aspects of the informatics field in which to specialize. The two-decade history of Community activity in this field is a record of trying all these options without being able to

Table 7.   Share by Region of Computer Hardware Market Held by Firms (per cent)

FIRM	REGION				
	West Europe	West Germany	United Kingdom	France	World Total
IBM	54.4	61.6	39.7	55.0	57.0
ICL	8.31	1.07	31.1	3.0	3.0
Unidata	8.82	17.6	—	10.0	2.7
Honeywell	10.22	7.0	9.6	15.0	9.0
Others	7.26	5.5	6.7	8.2	6.0

Note: Unidata, dissolved in 1975 was composed of: Philips (Netherlands), Siemens (West Germany), and CII (France). Sales by each member are recorded as sales by that firm in its own country.
Source: 3rd Data Processing Programme of the Federal Government (West Germany), 1976–9.

achieve programme clarity or garner the member support required for their implementation.

American MNEs active in informatics received their initial boost from systems analysis techniques pioneered by NASA and the Department of Defense (DOD), in the early 1960s.[19] The American government was the single largest producer and developer of computers and related equipment, disbursing more money than all members of the Community combined to sustain this effort. In addition to this support, government funds were disbursed in a secondary fashion which allowed technological innovations to become available to the entire market after the successful contractor had a chance to develop its product.[20] In order to enhance domestic competition these funds were disbursed to numerous American firms essentially in order to minimize the dominant position and potential of IBM. As a result IBM's share of the United States public market was only about 36 per cent as compared to its 68 per cent share of the total domestic market.[21]

The dominant position of IBM was therefore based only partly on this American contractual assistance. Instead IBM assumed its major global role for two other reasons. First, the majority of IBM products were financed by internal profits, a method which did away with the requirement to share its technological breakthroughs if generated as a result of governmental contractual assistance. Second, the global marketing system of IBM was not only extensive but also based on captive markets resulting from the firm's innovative leasing of hardware and sale of only compatible software. Thus in 1974 IBM employed 292,000 people worldwide with self-financing of $2,726 million. In comparison the largest European manufacturer, ICL of the United Kingdom, employed 29,200 with self-financing of $34 million.[22] In contrast to the American system of using contracts to create a pool of know-how for the entire industrial sector, European governments consistently directed contracts and funds to their national champions. Since this usually meant only one firm in each state the effect was to fragment available regional resources in pursuit of a national capability bereft of the ability to compete on a regional let alone a global scale. As Table 7 notes this system of government support did allow each of the major European states to support its own national industries, thereby minimizing IBM's share of their public sector markets. But IBM's dominance is clearly demonstrated when total European market shares are compared. Thus by the early 1970s the issues of American MNE dominance in computers and the need to develop a European industrial response had been defined and solutions were now sought simultaneously at national and Community levels.

With the exception of the short-lived Unidata venture, national responses assumed one of two avenues: to consolidate national firms within a programme such as the French Plan Calcul or to seek co-operative ventures with American firms.[23] The former ensured national control over an essential sector of domestic economic policy but at the expense of an internationally orientated competitive capability. The latter allowed European firms to share in American technological innovations and provided sales access to the United States market at the cost of junior status for the European partner. The period of the 1970s saw numerous examples of both options but with little permanent success. Several reasons may be suggested for these failures. Foremost is the small scale under which European firms laboured, even in cooperative ventures. The second is the lack of clarity over the areas in which to compete. To suggest the ability to compete in all aspects of informatics was to stretch already scarce resources to the point of failure. To focus on specific aspects, such as peripherals, was to acknowledge the inability to compete across the board. Finally, and perhaps uppermost, was the continued and unabated predominance of IBM in all areas. Once IBM had entered an area its marketing system effectively served to exclude others from those opportunities. Indeed the major restraint facing IBM's expansion was not competition from other firms but rather American and European anti-trust prosecution for abuse of a dominant market position. Ultimately the failure of these national efforts combined with the need to respond to continued, externally generated MNE pressure persuaded the Community to undertake a series of action programmes designed to achieve regional cooperation in the field of informatics and related applications.

A response to the foreign MNE: the 1973 and 1976 data processing programmes

In late 1973, as an integral part of its efforts to combat American MNE dominance in Community industrial sectors, the Commission proposed it first data processing programmes.[24] The objective was quickly to secure a 6 per cent share of the total world market which would then enable the Community to establish a 'fully viable and competitive European based computer industry by 1980'.[25] The programme outlined the various means to secure that objective. First, while industrial unification remained the long-term goal, because of competing national corporate groups the short-term objective was to promote 'limited collaboration' within the industry.[26] Second, to build up the domestic market for computers by encouraging the study of applications, in other words to promote an awareness of the benefits achievable through increased business and government utilization of computer technology. Finally, in view of the large increase in the 'peripheral' equipment sector, including integrated circuits, to stress aid to this industrial area where the present market was shared equally by European and American manufacturers.[27]

The obstacles to this programme were identical to those which had initially created the secondary status of European computer firms in global markets. First, the barrier raised by the use of different languages which, in turn, aided the captive market enjoyed by IBM. The solution of a Community language, along the lines of the introduction of COBOL by the American government, was impractical given the independent marketing and production of leading European firms, including ICL. Second, the continuing problem raised by discriminatory national procurement policies limited the accessibility of the non-IBM share of the market to their own domestic firms. Finally, the Community was unable to provide sufficient funds to cover even part of the proposal. Thus the Community recommended that the present system of national aids be continued with the addition of Community funds for special European-orientated projects.[28] Specific measures to implement this programme would follow as soon as the Council accepted the need for such an independent European data processing capability. On 15 July 1974, the Council did accept the programme and called for joint Community and member financing to ensure that by the early 1980s 'there is a fully viable and competitive European-based industry in all the fields concerned'.[29]

A European Parliament report on the data processing industry agreed with the thrust of the programme but felt it was not specific enough on certain critical points. After describing European companies as 'dwarfs' in comparison with American MNE's, its main point was that the 6 per cent share of the world market sought by the Commission programme was well below the 8–10 per cent mark suggested by experts as minimal to assure a profitable venture.[30] As a result the Parliament recommendation was not to concentrate on the impractical creation of a viable European industry, but rather to seek greater collaboration with American data processing firms. The Parliament envisaged a Community role in the development of common financial and other incentive measures to increase the attractiveness of European firms to potential American suitors. Central to this Community role was the need to act quickly in order to offset the emerging desire of members to protect and assist the commercial opportunities of their own firms to the exclusion or at least the minimization of any coordinated regional response.

It was not until 1976 that the Commission published its major proposal to fulfil the mandate of a 'viable European-based computer industry by 1980'. Acknowledging the interrelationship of the three basic industries in the field, data processing, telecommunications and electronic components, the Commission's initial premise was that a European capability in all areas was essential. Two themes were basic to the pursuit of the policy's objectives: first, the development of standards, procurement policies and allied programmes to maximize product choice, thereby increasing sales through expanded market demand; second, the promotion of joint incentives by European firms in newly developing areas including software, peripherals and office systems.

The major innovation proposed in the manner of directing aid to this programme was the introduction of the Community Premium Scheme, designed to fund projects proposed by consortia of Community firms in any of the areas covered by the initiative.[31] The Premium Scheme was apparently an attempt to revive the Community Development Contract in a more acceptable form since the committee that was to dispense these funds would have equal representation from region and state alike. The Premium Scheme provided that when the level of Community financing was 8 per cent of the worth of a project, consortia members were required to share the 'know-how' developed under the contract with other Community firms. In effect an effort was being made to redirect the manner of regional and state assistance to make it more commensurate with the successful secondary aid policy pioneered by the United States for its own firms. The total funds available to the programme were to be 30 million units of account over a period of four years, a sum equal to about 5 per cent of the required research and development if this project was to increase its present modest share of the available market.[32] It was expected that Community funds would serve as 'seed' money, and would be essentially worthless unless augmented by national assets. In sum, harmonization of Community data processing capability was being indirectly sought through the sales opportunities that were expected to redound from a pooling not only of assets but also of outcomes and applications.

Needless to repeat this comprehensive and optimistic programme failed to materialize and the reality of Community action and stature in data processing remains far removed from the hopes inherent in the 1976 programme. Although parts of that initiative were reworked and absorbed into later programmes, nothing resembling a Community response to this technological challenge was able to emerge. As Table 8 notes, Europe's position in these technologies has continued to decline over the past few years. One author has gone so far as to ask if 'Europe [will] be relegated at the end of the century to the category of former industrialized countries?'[33] His response that 'a new lease of life is still

Table 8. World market in electric and electronic materials: Europe's deteriorating position

World Trade (current $ m)	1978	1979	1980	1981	1982
	105,439	125,464	151,252	157,084	159,652
Share of world market held by:					
France	6.5	6.9	6.4	5.7	5.4
Germany	15.9	15.2	13.9	12.0	12.0
Italy	4.5	4.6	4.5	4.0	4.1
Netherlands	4.8	4.7	4.2	3.5	3.6
UK	7.0	7.1	7.5	6.6	6.6
EEC	*42.6*	*42.5*	*40.4*	*35.7*	*34.9*
EFTA	7.0	7.1	6.6	6.0	6.0
USA	17.9	18.2	19.4	20.5	21.6
JAPAN	18.1	16.9	17.9	21.6	20.7
Asia*	8.4	8.8	9.2	9.8	10.2
Other industrialised countries†	2.8	3.2	3.3	3.5	3.4

* Except Japan, China, Korea, North Korea, Mongolia, Vietnam
† Spain, Canada, Australia, New Zealand
Source: FIEE, quoted in Michel Richonnier, 'Europe's Decline is not Irreversible', *Journal of Common Market Studies*, 22,3 (March 1984), p. 228.

possible within a European framework' will be further developed in the discussion of the Esprit project in Chapter 5.[34]

The Community and aerospace policy

Excluding certain heavily subsidized military aircraft projects such as the French Mirage and the joint Anglo-German–Italian Tornado, no other national or European collaborative airline venture had been successful prior to the 1980s. Instead Western Europe, like the rest of the world, purchased American aircraft for almost all of its civilian needs. This is not to suggest that certain sectors of the European industry were not commercially profitable. Indeed in airframe design and in the development of jet engines European manufacturers were comparable to their American counterparts, if not slightly advanced. In fact many of the aerospace systems presently in world-wide use are the result of initial design developments by European firms.[35] Just as certainly their production in a commercially viable sense had inevitably been the result of action by American multinationals.

A competitive market requires that firms adapt their structures to changing conditions in order to assure the most profitable use of materials and resources. In aerospace the period from 1970 to 1975 was such a time of market restructuring, with industry and community projections suggesting three roughly equal global sales markets (see Table 9). Although global plane sales continued to increase, the phasing out of the Vietnam conflict and the NASA space effort meant a lessening of the possible contracts available to American firms. American MNE response was a 32.3 per cent decrease in employed personnel which allowed firm productivity to remain constant.[36] The outcome of this restructuring ensured that American products would be competitively priced and, indeed, these firms made even greater inroads into foreign markets to make up for the loss of domestic sales.[37]

Community manufacturers proved less able or willing to adapt to this period of restructuring. During the same 1970–5 period aerospace employment in Europe dropped by only 7 per cent due mainly to the consolidation of British airlines into one new national firm, British Airways.[38] According to one industry survey the result was that European productivity now stood at about one-third to two-thirds that of their American competitors. Translated into the ability to compete profitably in an open market it meant even less sales for European firms. In 1974 Western Europe, with a sales market of about 25 per cent of the world's total, purchased 99 per cent of its planes from the United States, with domestic manufacturers supplying the remaining 1 per cent.[39]

Even though remaining dependent on government support European manufacturers continually sought partnerships with other firms to better their competitive posture through cooperation. Three possible collaborative ventures were open to Community firms: cooperation with an American or other foreign firm; agreement with other Community companies; or to cater solely to national contracts and

Table 9. Aircraft Markets by Region

	Europe	United States	Rest of the World
Commision	30%	35%	35%
Association Européenne de Constructeurs de Matériel Aérospatial (AECMA)	22%	36%	42%

Source: EC Commision, *Action Programme for the European Aeronautical Sector*, 3 October 1975 (Brussels: EC Bulletin Supplement 11/75), p. 23.

requirements. One may suggest in descending order of priority the attractions underlying each of these options. First was the need to maintain a domestic defence industry capable of meeting state-defined requirements. Such a national position could range from the total independence of France, through shared efforts such as the Tornado, to the Belgian, Dutch and Danish position of near complete dependence on foreign products. Indeed the perceived level of national prestige reflected in the ability to maintain an independent capability is often used to sustain production of a craft long after its justification on competitive grounds has passed.[40]

The second reason to seek a partner is the issue of profitability. Since purchases within the United States and Western Europe are heavily weighted in favour of a domestic product, other factors such as price, reliability and maintenance being equal, a consortium can reasonably assume that its sales chances will increase with every new country included in the venture.[41] The ability to secure new sources of financing and to eliminate duplicative ventures is also an outcome of cooperation. The final justification is the idea to create some form of European air industry that could compete successfully against American MNEs. Central to this objective was the ability to aggregate state and regional aid to a sector that suffered from undercapitalization and compartmentalization in comparison to American companies (see Table 10). Not only did the primary method of dispensing assistance fragment the Community's industrial structure into separate production compartments, but even when regional and national assets were combined the total fell far short of that available to American firms. In 1975 alone

Table 10. National Government Aid to the European
Aerospace Industry (in million UA for 1975
$1=1.25 UA)

Research and Development	Civil	Military
FRG	47.7	462.9
Belgium	1.8	.1
France	148.4	359.6
Italy	1.6	21.2
Netherlands	.9	1.8
UK	119.5	305.6
Total	319.9	1,151.2

Source: EC Commision, *Directorate General for Internal Market and Industrial Affairs—Data on the Aeronautical Sector*, 2 August 1977 (Brussels: SEC [77] 2939), Table 43.

American assistance to its aerospace industry was about 11,000 million units of account (UA), as compared to total European aid of about 3,600 million UA.[42] Clearly some basic restructuring and not merely an aggregation of resources was required.

The Commission's response: the 1975 proposal for a unified European aerospace industry

The 1975 action programme for the aeronautical sector was a direct outcome of the measures first proposed in the 1970 industrial policy, and was designed to maintain an independent European global commercial capability in this advanced technology, employment-intensive, prestige sector.[43] To accomplish this objective the Commission proposed to consolidate distinct and often duplicative national industries into a single Community system capable of directly meeting the competition afforded by the American MNEs.

The programme recognized the necessity of shifting from a primary to a secondary form of assistance distribution if the present fragmentation in the market was to be eliminated. As important was the recognition that restructuring and not merely realignment of domestic purchasing habits was essential if the Community market was to serve as a foundation from which industry could then branch out into the global market. If the market alone was to be responsible for such realignment then, based on its past record, there was little hope of success. Thus the Commission had to assume an initiatory role to submerge national disputes in pursuit of maintaining a regional aerospace capability that could become competitive in global markets.

The 1975 aerospace policy was quite explicit in its objectives. Sponsorship of the European aerospace industry was to be taken from national control so that even intergovernmental cooperation between national firms, as practiced in the Airbus consortia, would not be acceptable. Instead, 'sponsorship of the aircraft industry would be exercised by the Community'.[44] The means to implement this programme were as explicitly stated:

(1) consolidataion of all major civil programmes;
(2) a joint basic research programme;
(3) introduction of a system of Community financing;
(4) development of a common export strategy to penetrate foreign markets.[45]

These objectives were an extension of those first proposed by the 1970 industrial policy. Commissioner Spinelli, as the author of both the aerospace programme and the industrial policy, expressed the continuity between both proposals when he stated, 'that the only way an aircraft industry can survive in any European country is by becoming truly European'.[46]

The major propositions of the aerospace programme may be quite easily summarized. First, joint financing and research and development grants were to be channelled through the Community, thereby replacing the present fragmented system of national assistance to domestic firms. Second, a joint procurement agency to consolidate projects and purchases in the military sector was to be established. Third, an increase in civilian sector productivity was sought through adoption of American MNE operational techniques with respect to both firm–state and inter-firm relations. Finally, European marketing efforts were to be concentrated in the non-American market area which was expected to account for 65 per cent of all sales in the period from 1975 to 1995 (see Table 11).

The programme was not presented as being anti-American, but rather as a means to seek equality with the United States by means of a united European capability with the resources and backing to place it on a competitive par with foreign firms. It was a programme based on the realities of the market and the recognition that competitiveness was tied closely to the assistance measures made possible by regional direction of resources and opportunities. To suggest, as did the French Prime Minister, that shares of the available market should be guaranteed by international agreement was totally opposite to the spirit of the Commission's proposal.[47] Instead the Commission was proposing that

Table 11. Commision and Industrial Projections for Aircraft, 1975–85 (in millions of dollars at 1974 prices)

	Hypothesis I		Hypothesis II	
	Commission	AECMA	Commission	AECMA
Short- and medium-haul aircraft	+ 19	+1,964.7	−2,698	−1,010.0
Long-haul aircraft	−986	−2,373.7	−2,708	−2,914.7
Total	−967	− 490.0	−5,406	−3,924.7

Hypothesis I is the result of a combination of high forecasts for traffic and market penetration, and Hypothesis II is the result of a combination of low forecasts for traffic market penetration

Note: Commission figures for Hypothesis I and II are 30.4 per cent and 13.1 per cent respectively of the world market. For AECMA the comparable figures are 19.4 per cent and 12.8 per cent of the world market.

Source: EC Commission, *The Community's Industrial Policy*, p. 22.

market shares could be secured only by the manufacture of a competitive product, which necessitated the merger of separate national capabilities into a regional whole. Adoption and implementation of its aerospace proposal would therefore only be the first step in that restructuring process.

The 1975 aerospace policy was never implemented, joining the 1976 informatics initiative as one more Community programme failure. But unlike in the informatics sector, regional success in aerospace has been accomplished through the Airbus consortium. Established in 1974, Airbus sought to produce a competitive family of aircraft by coordinating the resources and marketing practices of its members, France, the Netherlands, Spain, West Germany and the United Kingdom.[48] Initially heavily dependent on state assistance, Airbus emerged in the 1980s as a true global competitor on a par with any of its American competitors. The reasons for its success will be discussed in Chapter 5, but it is sufficient to note at this point that the Community's inability to fashion regional programmes in these vital high-technology sectors served to continue the perceived technology gap between the United States and Europe in a fashion that makes current harmonization initiatives more palatable and thus more acceptable because of that previous legacy of failure.

NOTES

1. Mira Wilkins, *The Emergence of the Multinational Enterprise* (Cambridge, MA: Harvard University Press, 1970).
2. Lawrence Franco, *The European Multinationals* (London: Harper and Row, 1976).
3. D. Swann and D. McLachlan, *Concentration or Competition: A European Dilemma?*, European series no. 1 (London: PEP, 1967).
4. J.-J. Servan-Schreiber, *The American Challenge* (New York: Avon Books, 1967), p. 40.
5. Raymond Vernon, 'MNE-Power v. Sovereignty', *Foreign Affairs*, 49 (April 1971), p. 736.
6. Swann and McLachlan, op. cit., p. 6.
7. Roland Drago, 'Public Enterprise in France', in W. G. Friedmann and J. F. Garner, eds, *Government and Enterprise* (New York: Columbia University Press, 1970).
8. Swann and McLachlan, op. cit., p. 26.
9. *EC Bulletin*, March 1967, p. 23.
10. *EC Bulletin*, February 1970, pp 9–14.
11. 'That's UNIDATA, that was', *The Economist*, 13 September 1975, p. 6.
12. *EC Bulletin*, September 1972, pp. 77–84.
13. EC Commission, *The Community's Industrial Policy*, 18 March 1970 (Brussels: EC Bulletin Supplement 4/1970), p. 14.
14. *EC Bulletin*, December 1976, pp. 22–3.
15. EC Commission, *The Community's Industrial Policy*, p. 19.

16. European Parliament Working Document, *Report on the Proposal for a Regulation setting up a European Export Bank*, 4 May 1977, Doc. 66/77, PE 42.970.
17. *Official Journal of the European Communities*, no. C299/2, 18 November 1980, no. 4411.171.
18. EC Commission, *The Community's Industrial Policy*, p. 4.
19. EC Commission, *A Four-Year Programme for the Development of Informatics in the Community*, COM(76) 524 final, 29 October 1976, vol. III, p. 127 (hereafter *Informatics Study*).
20. See later discussion on state aid to industry in the United States and in Western Europe.
21. *Informatics Study*, vol. I, p. 5.
22. *Informatics Study*, vol. III, p. 77.
23. 'France's Electronics Strategy: The Americans Know Best', *The Economist*, 18 November 1978, p. 119.
24. European Parliament Working Document, *Report on a Community Policy on Data Processing*, 2 July 1974, Doc. 153/74, PE 36.983, pp. 1–32.
25. Ibid., p. 5.
26. Ibid., p. 29.
27. Ibid., pp. 8–12.
28. 'EEC View of Preference', *The Times*, 20 February 1973, p. 20.
29. Official Journal of the European Communities, *Council Resolution on a Community Policy on Data Processing*, no. C86/1, 20 July 1974.
30. European Parliament Working Document, *Report on a Community Policy on Data Processing*.
31. 'Proposal for a Council Resolution on the Community Premium Scheme for the Data Processing Sector', *Informatics Study*, vol. I, pp. 40–6 and Article 14.
32. Ibid., pp. 19–22.
33. Michel Richonnier, 'Europe's Decline is not Irreversible', *Journal of Common Market Studies*, 22, 3 (March 1984), p. 228.
34. Ibid.
35. European Parliament Working Document, *Interim Report for an Action Programme for the European Aeronautical Sector*, 5 July 1976, Doc. 203/76, PE 43.158, p. 40.
36. 'U.S. Airlines Ahead in Productivity', *The Times*, 30 March 1977, p. 23.
37. EC Commission, *Directorate General for Internal Market and Industrial Affairs—Data on the Aeronautical Sector*, 2 August 1977, SEC (77) 2939, p 55.
38. 'Taking Good Care of Them', *The Economist*, 22 July 1972, p. 62.
39. 'RR Technicians Favour Joint Deal with Boeing Rather than European', *The Times*, 4 July 1978, p. 24.
40. 'A Continental Planemaker Under Stress', *The Times*, 6 October 1977, p. 23.
41. 'Britain's Aero Groups Call for Link-up as Rivals to Americans', *The Times*, 5 December 1975, p. 18.
42. EC Commission, *The Community's Industrial Policy*, p. 21.
43. EC Commission, *Action Programme for the European Aeronautical Sector*, 3 October 1975 (Brussels: EC Bulletin Supplement 11/75), pp. 1–33.
44. Ibid., p. 11.
45. European Parliament Working Document, *Report on European Armaments Procurement Cooperation*, 8 May 1978, Doc. 83/78, PE 50.944.
46. 'Fly European', *The Economist*, 5 June 1976, p. 84.
47. 'Warning on the Threat of U.S. Monopoly', *The Times*, 7 July 1977, p. 24.
48. 'Six European Groups to Concentrate on Building New Airlines for 1970s', *The Times*, 7 September 1975, p. 28.

4 Structural obstacles to new Community responses

It is a persistent irony that the primary rationale for European unity, that of economic cooperation, has been unable to redress a continuing erosion of the Community in the global commercial environment.[1] This is not to suggest a diminution of the Community's share of international trade. Indeed the Community continues as the world's largest trading area, a position that should be maintained in the future. It is rather in the nature of trading items that the failure is apparent. Consistently the Community has been unable to make the transition, as the United States and Japan are doing, into those high-technology sectors which are essential to the foundation and substance of European economic objectives (see Table 12). Although individual members continue in the forefront of global research and development and innovations, it is glaringly apparent that such efforts are unable to match the resources of the United States or the single-mindedness of the Japanese. Three areas in particular, arms sales, technology transfers and export controls, continue to plague the Community's ability to redress this imbalance in pursuit of security policy harmonization for the region.

THE ARTIFICIAL SEPARATION BETWEEN DEFENCE AND ECONOMIC PRODUCTION

Chapter 3 detailed the role of the American MNE in inhibiting the ability of European firms to aggregate their resources and objectives in pursuit of opportunities in the production and sale of high-technology goods. Whether in aerospace, data processing or the application of innovations, American MNEs were able to assume dominant positions based on their leadership in the three factors of marketing essential for global success: corporate control through direct investment; profes-

Table 12. Trade balances for high-technology goods 1970 and 1982 (billions of dollars)

	EEC		USA		Japan	
	1970	1982	1970	1982	1970	1982
EEC						
Imports from	—	—	−2.4	−13.9	−0.4	− 8.2
Exports to	—	—	+2.2	+10.5	+0.3	+ 1.7
Balance			−0.2	− 3.4	−0.1	− 6.5
USA						
Imports from	−2.2	−10.5	—	—	−1.9	−20.8
Exports to	+2.4	+13.9	—	—	+0.9	+ 4.9
Balance	+0.2	+ 3.4			−1.0	−15.9
Japan						
Imports from	−0.3	− 1.7	−0.9	− 4.9	—	—
Exports to	+0.4	+ 8.2	+1.9	+20.8	—	—
Balance	+0.1	+ 6.5	+1.0	+15.9		

Source: B. Cardiff, Commission of the European Communities, February 1984 figures based on import data clf).

sional management; and market control through product innovation. Central to the success of these firms had been their ability to benefit from American defence requirements. Defence research and development in high-technology areas provided the basis for American firms to exploit findings for commercial applications. The early lead of American computer firms was largely based on the needs of the Department of Defense (DOD) and the follow-on exploitation of results for business use. This opportunity to pursue 'dual use' of defence-related research and development is derived from the American government system of directing assistance to firms, which differs substantially from that used in Europe.

American government assistance is in the form of research and development funds, development contracts and military procurement policies which are offered to industry as a whole through the procedures of open bids on particular projects. A specific firm is awarded the contract and sole responsibility for the work. After a specified period of time any technological developments resulting from American government contracts must be shared with other domestic manufacturers. Barriers such as the Buy American Act and the need to shelter sensitive defence projects have served effectively to bar foreign companies from entering this lucrative market.[2] As a result a pool of knowledge is established with domestic competition serving as the inducement to refine the new technology and get it into production as quickly and as inexpensively as possible. Since this government assistance is not directed to a specific firm but is, instead, designed to produce further refinements from the initial research, it will be termed 'secondary aid'.

In contrast European assistance is in the form of government grants and research and development funding normally given directly to a national firm for use on a specific project or for a technological refinement of an already existing product. The fact that all European aerospace manufacturers, most data processing firms, as well as all security-active companies are public enterprises allows the government easily to compartmentalize such assistance. In this fashion resources are distributed by departments charged with responsibility for specific industrial sectors, rather than more broadly through general grants to support research for an industry as a whole. This situation is compounded within the Community, where twelve separate governments pursue this method of dispensing assistance. Even when a European consortium to produce a specific product is established, the concept of 'fair return' on investment ensures that product innovations remain the province of the national team whose responsibility it was to complete that portion of the work. Such assistance going directly from government to specific firm will be termed 'primary aid', to distinguish it from the secondary aid offered by the American system.

The differences between primary and secondary aid translate into competitive differences in the market-place. First, secondary aid creates a pool of knowledge for the industry as a whole and encourages its use in both the commercial and defence sectors. Primary aid, instead, is limited to a single firm or product, which minimizes its effectiveness for dual applications or even sectoral utilization. Further, secondary aid maximizes the impact of such assistance by spreading it across the industry as a whole, rather than dividing it into compartments, such as civil-military or national as opposed to regional firms. The objective of secondary aid is, therefore, to increase the applicability of new technology, in effect creating new demand for the design and the product. Third, secondary aid allows all manufacturers access to the same technological information after a specified period where the initial contractor may exploit his winning bid. Assuming an equal ability to translate that information into specific products the dividing line between competing designs will be how well they serve purchaser and market requirements. Designs that do not are dropped while the successful product is assured of substantial support and, therefore, of sales. This winnowing of competitors results in longer production runs at lower cost and higher profits which can then be translated into an advantage in the international market-place. Primary aid going direct from government to firm does not require the firm to assess the needs or desires of its potential customers, nor is there any inter-firm competition to refine designs into saleable products. Fourth, secondary aid allows the government to remain clear of industry decisions on how employment policies are to be revamped in light of a successful or unsuccessful product design. Primary aid binds the industry to the government and begins to blur the distinction between a competitive product and a project under the heading of public interest. Employment policies take on a value all their own under the latter heading. Finally, primary aid shifts what should be decision according to competitive norms to policy-making according to governmental direction. The result is that continuation or abandonment of a specific project becomes a politicized issue. Interest groups and party units already active at governmental level may simply extend their competence to include what otherwise would be a decision by the industry itself. This is naturally an extension of the directed economy that is more prevalent in Europe than in the United States and must therefore be seen in those terms, although trends such as privatization and comprehensive industrial policies might begin to blur these traditionally distinct approaches.

There are two other factors that distinguish the domestic support potential for MNEs extended by the American and European governments. First is the nature of the domestic market itself. While one might suggest that both the Community and the United States have a similar number of major security-active firms and, therefore, imply similar approaches to the domestic market, this would be an incorrect appraisal of actual conditions in both regions. While American manufacturers maintain a healthy domestic rivalry among themselves they do so behind government barriers such as the Buy American Act. The Act gives American industry a 50 per cent price advantage on defence products and a 6 per cent advantage on civilian goods, effectively serving to bar rival foreign firms from competing profitably in the American domestic market. Second is the fact that government influence may be used in order to help close a transaction for domestic firms. The fact that ex-colonial Africa purchases most of its aircraft from France is a latent indication of governmental intervention on behalf of its domestic manufacturers. A more patent act of aid was the 1975 agreement of the American government to purchase a large quantity of Belgian machine-guns if, in turn, Belgium would join Denmark, the Netherlands and Norway in choosing the American F-16 over the French Mirage in a major purchase by these European NATO members.[3] In summary, then, the global standing of American MNEs may be directly traced to the manner by which government research and development assistance is dispensed and to the dual use made of generated findings.

Community acknowledgement of competitive shortcomings in such technologies has led to the realization of the need to direct research and development funding along the lines followed by the American government. Directives on public contracts and the need to rationalize procurement policies have existed for many years and will be discussed in a separate section. It is the second factor, that of dual use, that has only recently been opened to discussion.[4]

National defence structures, treaty limits and fragmented public opinion have coalesced to ensure that security issues have not been brought within the Community's decision-making mandate. Coopera-tion on selected defence projects, such as Tornado, remain under member control. Research and development funding, procurement decisions and sales opportunities are directed by member military organizations. Neither sharing of results nor cooperation in sales priorities enters the equation. Cooperation in manufacturing is just that, as sales are viewed as an open system with partners competing for available markets. Although profits on ventures such as Tornado are distributed to consortium members on a pro rata basis it is but one of the products marketed by Community firms. In the existing system separate national defence structures and requirements ensure competi-tion between members to support their domestic capability through the expedient of foreign sales. These sales receipts in turn permit longer production runs and allow state military forces to fill their require-ments at less overall cost. This direct economic benefit, when wedded to the political limits placed on the Community's role in security policy, have increased overt competition between members, decreased the efficient use of available resources and diminished national ability to translate product innovations into more marketable commercial uses. This production fragmentation and the further lack of standardi-zation also limit the European ability to compete with the United States in meeting NATO sales requirements. Thus short-term economic gains mandated by limited and separate national economies have prevented political cooperation or even aggregation of assets to benefit both Community–Third World and Community–American sales opportunities. This continued compartmentalization of defence and commercial projects has been strongly criticized by the Commission and Parliament as inimical to political cooperation and wasteful of available economic resources. It is the latter factor that has lent new support at national and Community levels to renewed interest in pursuing the possibility of defence and procurement cooperation within the framework of the Community's existing and projected industrial policy objectives.

The original impetus to eliminating the discreteness between defence and economic issues was the 1978 Klepsch Report.[5] Among its specific recommendations was the:

(1) creation of a single Community market in military equipment;
(2) acknowledgement of the interrelationship of civilian and military production sectors;
(3) pursuit of the development of an overall Community industrial policy;
(4) integration of these Community efforts into the sales exchange of the NATO 'two-way' street;
(5) creation of a European Armament Procurement Agency (EAPA) to act under Community control to direct these varied but interrelated activities.

On 14 June 1978 the Parliament requested the Commission to develop and submit to the Council a new action programme 'for the development and production of conventional armaments within the framework of a common industrial policy'.[6] To assist that initiative David Greenwood, Director of the Centre for Defence Studies at Aberdeen, was commissioned to prepare a report designed to promote defence cooperation among Community members. Greenwood's report was delivered in 1980, and, together with the earlier Klepsch study, has established the general parameters for subsequent discussion.[7] While concerned with the same issue the two reports diverged widely on policy recommendations. Klepsch's proposal for a European Armament Procurement Agency (EAPA) with central responsibility is far more integrationist than the modest information clearing-house suggested by Greenwood's European Defence Analysis Bureau (EADA). In addition Greenwood rejected as unrealistic in the short term Klepsch's suggestions for resource and production consolidation to eliminate waste by duplication, as well as the rationalization of military requirements to allow more sales within the regional market, thereby lessening the need to export to survive. Greenwood later suggested that the lack of discussion by the Council of Klepsch's study was due to lack of support for its suggestions which made his own modest but attainable recommendations all the more attractive.[8]

There has been no resolution yet which might suggest which of the two proposals might be favoured by the Community and individual members. Instead current initiatives were prompted by a May 1981 speech by Commission Vice President Tugendhat, designed to refocus attention on the underlying problems and away from acrimony over the specific Klepsch and Greenwood suggestions.[9] This effort to present alternatives and to synthesize previous suggestions culminated in the 1983 Fergusson Report, entitled *Arms Procurement within a Common Industrial Policy*.[10] It is this report that is most often cited as the basis for renewed interest in tackling the issue of a Community production policy for security matters. The heart of the report's recommendations are encompassed in a single sentence: 'Defence purchasing is the single most important field where action is required to ensure that European industries, especially in the area of information technologies, shall be able not only to compete with the United States and Japanese firms but shall also be able to strengthen Europe's own defence capability.'[11] Three interrelated ingredients are identified in this prescription, the completion of which is essential to the success of security-orientated initiatives for the Community. Foremost is the need to develop a common policy for Community arms sales.[12] While most Community members are exporters of arms the principals are France, Britain, West Germany, Italy, the Netherlands and Belgium. Total Community arms exports average about 50 per cent of those of the United States. Of this total the French share is about 50 per cent, the British nearly 25 per cent, with the balance spread among the remaining Community members.[13] Although export sales policies vary by state two factors are common to all member programmes. First is the need to export because the limited requirements of national forces cannot financially support the research and development and manufacturing base essential to modern and technologically orientated weapon systems. Second is the distinct lack of criteria to determine the suitability of a potential purchaser. With the possible exception of West Germany's acknowledged need to fulfil its 'historical responsibility toward the Jewish people', few other constraints are present to limit member export sales or policies.[14] This has resulted in sales to mostly volatile regions such as the Middle East, where desire for modern weapons is driven by oil revenues and local tensions often to the exclusion of more rational calculations of need. Most members, whether from a moral perspective or as a response to domestic political pressure, would like to eliminate or minimize these sales and thereby decrease the leverage potential of these purchasers over their policies. To limit exports in an effort to minimize such regional tensions would simply redound to the detriment of Community producers and their dependent national defence structures, since the vacuum would likely be filled by alternative suppliers such as the United States or the Soviet Union. Therefore to accomplish this objective there must exist an alternative market outlet to allow the continued and needed influx of revenues now garnered from Third World sales. This requirement, according to Fergusson, could be met through the adoption of a common European arms sales policy. Fergusson reaffirmed the Dankert Report of 1977 on arms procurement prepared for the Western European Union (WEU) which stated that: 'Members of the Atlantic Alliance provide an arms market large enough for economic production that would be independent of exports to the Third World.'[15] Fergusson continues and concludes that: 'a rational arms procurement policy will eliminate the need of Community arms manufacturers to look outside the Alliance for their survival.'[16] The adoption of such a harmonized export programme would then directly support the second ingredient of the Fergusson report, the need for European firms to compete in high-technology competition against the United States and Japan. Putting aside for the moment the very real political obstacles to such an economic agreement there is persuasive evidence to support the view that such a 'Community programme for the development and production of armaments would have multiple effects throughout a whole range of important industrial sectors'.[17] Such a policy of export cooperation, whether or not combined with national specialization in particular production areas, would lead to spill-over from shared defence initiatives to other high-technology sectors such as microelectronics, aerospace and telecommunications. An additional benefit would be the increased availability of joint European products which could then be used to make more equitable the NATO two-way street which now dramatically favours the United States to the tune of $1,183 as against Europe's $125 million.[18] While not able completely to minimize European dependence on the United States for large-scale programmes such as Trident, cooperative development of systems at lower levels would enhance the economic and political standing of European members with respect to the United States. These developments would then complete the objectives defined by the Fergusson Report, essentially the use of arms cooperation in procurement and development to support European political cohesion in pursuit of a comprehensive security policy.

The Fergusson prescriptions are just that, a coherent set of economic proposals to redress a very real imbalance in high-technology capability between the Community and the United States. The political obstacles to their immediate implementation or even acceptance are enormous. But these obstacles should not require them to be dismissed as mere fantasy and therefore destined to be shelved with their predecessors. For the prescriptions and their attendant political opportunities have become the focal points around which Community and member discussions have now coalesced. Although the report has not established the current agenda for discussion, its assumptions and recommendations are recognized as the guiding parameters for future action.

EXPORT CONTROLS, TECHNOLOGY TRANSFERS AND THE COMMUNITY

Integral to any analysis of harmonization efforts in the Community's production and sale of high-technology goods and processes is the issue of export controls.[19] Although national in origin, the interdependence of military and commercial technology and processes has, to a great extent, elevated this discussion beyond the plane of domestic politics. While economic in scope, export controls have increasingly come to be viewed, especially by recent American administrations, as instruments of an activist foreign policy. This assessment is amply substantiated when viewed through the prism of Afghanistan, Poland and Nicaragua. While acknowledged as the derivative sovereign right of a state, export controls have become increasingly troublesome because of their impact beyond national boundaries. Discussed under the term 'extraterritoriality', the economic interdependence of Western economies and firms, especially in the high-technology sectors, ensures that action in one state to control exports will have an effect on other states in that dyadic relationship.[20] The extent of that effect differs according to, and is dependent on, the nature, type and purpose of specific control measures. But within the ambit of Western economies with increasingly divergent views on the purpose of such controls any effect not subject to a right of national refusal is viewed as unacceptable. It is the coincidence of these differing economic perspectives and the accelerated use of export measures by the United States that accounts in large measure for the recent and heightened concern over the need to redress this problem.

Legal implications of export controls

It is a settled principle of Western international law that when national jurisdictions overlap an effort must be made to identify which states' interests are paramount and therefore to be given precedence. Few economic issues may be securely placed on the level of national security and therefore negotiations revolve about individual state assessments at lesser levels of priority. To complicate this lack of a standard measure of comparative concern, there are differing legal measures applicable to export-related issues. Even the routine definitions of what constitutes a corporation differ, with the Community moving toward the civil law theory of 'enterprise unity' and the United States steadfastly adhering to the incorporation-centred view of common law. The penetration of the Community by American MNEs has intensified the need to standardize these definitions both within the region and between it and foreign markets. While the definition of corporate identity is an aspect of export controls it is primarily a technical concern and therefore less important than the more comprehensive issue of extraterritorial application of national laws. This latter concept concerns the ability of one state to extend its legal and thus political control beyond its own boundaries. The dual taxation of American firms operating in the Common Market by their Internal Revenue Service is but one example of this issue.

The concept of extraterritoriality takes on added importance when economic issues are decided for essentially political reasons and enforcement then moves from the relatively simple sphere of legal off-sets to one of incompatible national objectives. Incompatibility of foreign, including economic, policies, is the basis for the current United States–Community disagreement over the use and application of export-related controls. While these issues such as agriculture often enter this arena it is the high-technology sector that remains at the heart of the controversy. The addition of an East–West focus imposed essentially by the recent American administration serves to increase both the stakes and the economic outcomes of the underlying disunity.

The application of conflicting legal approaches to exports was underscored by the activities associated with the 1982 gas-pipeline controversy. Politically directed by United States foreign policy objectives, American companies were prohibited from fulfilling existing contracts or pursuing future opportunities with firms constructing the 3,500-mile long pipeline from Urengoi in Western Siberia to Westhaus, West Germany. Although American firms such as Caterpillar lost present contracts and future 'goodwill', mostly to rival European and Japanese companies, no recourse was available given the acknowledged American right to impose such restrictions on its domestic business activities. Given the political underpinnings of the American boycott decision success was possible only if alternative supply sources were also forced to comply with these export restrictions. To bolster its decision the United States government sought to extend these export sanctions to foreign firms doing business under licence from already proscribed American companies.[21] In short, the American government was asking allied leaders to support its unilateral decision by limiting business opportunities open to their own firms. The response in France, West Germany and Britain was immediate with each state requiring its firms to comply with existing contracts and allowing them latitude to explore future business opportunities.[22] Pointing to continued American grain sales to the Soviet Union these states dismissed the Reagan administration's argument that completion of the pipeline would increase European dependence on Soviet supplies and create leverage over their future foreign policy options and stances. Although couching their arguments in these competitive terms it was actually the diverging views of economic and trade relations between the United States and the Community that formed the basis for the European refusal to comply. Export-orientated for survival rather than for mere profit, European governments were loath to dismiss lucrative market opportunities for the essentially unilateral and nationally derived position of an ally. No longer dependent on American economic sustenance, Europeans were hard pressed to comply with its demands, preferring instead the compromise solution implied in a dyad of equal powers.[23] The American recognition of the disappearance of hegemony in Alliance economic relations and the need for compromise rather than coercion was manifested in the recent revisions to American export controls that occurred after the initial crisis was terminated.

In compliance with President Reagan's original wishes the Commerce Department had on 22 June 1982 amended relevant sections of the Export Administration Act to expand American controls on the export and re-export of goods and processes related to oil, its exploitation and refinement.[24] The essence of the change was to prohibit persons and firms within third countries from re-exporting machinery or processes gained as a result of contracts, or through licence or other arrangements with American firms. These modifications were in addition to those already in place that affected all American firms no matter where situated. To encourage especially European adherence to American controls the severing of trade contacts with firms that refused to comply were included in amendments to the Export Administration Act. The United States justified the extension of national regulatory measures to foreign firms on the basis of 'national security', a position consistent with the political context of its overall actions.[25]

The response of European states affected by these changes was immediate and negative. The joint sentiment of individual European states was presented best in a position paper issued by the European Community on 12 August 1982.[26] Progressing from their shared position that, '[t]he American measures clearly infringe the principle of territoriality', the Community paper dismissed the Reagan administration's contention that these measures were required for reasons of national security. Noting that the measures were grounded on Section 6 of the Export Administration Act (foreign policy controls) and not on Section 5 (national security controls), the statement concluded: 'The United States Government itself . . . has not sought to base the Amendments on the considerations of national security.'[27] Clearly the Community's position reflected the essentially economic view that they had assumed concerning the original controversy and its policy effects on American statements. Based on this sense of competing economic perceptions the Community saw no need to comply with the American request and further viewed the action itself as an illegal interference with national and regional prerogatives to develop and control economic matters.

The determination of these European states to maintain the sanctity of already signed contracts, by requiring compliance in the face of American pressure, was an extension of their differing views on the nature and role of such export restrictions. The damage for the United States was felt not only by loss of business but also in the weakened ability of the administration to coerce or guide its partners toward common economic and strategic policies. Recognizing the perceptual loss of leadership that would result by continuing sanctions when alternative suppliers existed, the Reagan administration began to modify its objectives in the area of export controls. In 1984 the administration noted that embargoes of goods and processes would not be implemented unless strict compliance by all major suppliers could be guaranteed beforehand.[28] In a similar fashion new Commerce Department regulations went into effect on 1 January 1985, making it easier to sell personal computers to Eastern bloc states.[29] More recently proposed changes to American export laws would allow sales of previously sanctioned products if its firms can show availability of goods from allies with 'comparable quality and in such quantities that controlling them would no longer improve US national security'.[30] Notwithstanding these changes designed to ease economic loss to American firms in the face of non-compliance by foreign companies and governments, the Reagan administration still continues to adhere to a definition of export controls that allows extraterritorial application of United States rules when deemed to be in the country's best interest. This American position continues to be a sore point with European allies especially with regard to the use they might make of shared technology if they agree to join in the SDI project as partners with the United States.[31]

THE ROLE OF THE COORDINATING COMMITTEE CONSULTATIVE
GROUP (COCOM)

The issue of export controls is complicated further when products or
processes are 'dual use' in nature. In that instance both commercial
and defence organizations become enmeshed in what often becomes
an exercise in pursuit of divergent institutional objectives. Although
simplistic to repeat, it is none the less essential to underscore that the
United States Departments of Commerce and Defense view the issue of
technology transfers from different and often incompatible perspectives.[32] Protection of security versus the promotion of commerce often
ensures that Departmental positions differ on the wisdom of specific
transfers. These differences, in turn, create disagreements within
COCOM, the Alliance committee designed to monitor sales to Eastern
Europe and the Soviet Union.[33]

COCOM is the primary mechanism for export supervision and
includes all NATO members with the exception of Spain and with the
addition of Japan.[34] The Western European reliance on exports for
survival plus natural commercial partnerships with Eastern Europe
have resulted in less willingness on its part to increase the number of
items subject to COCOM transfer restrictions. This divergence of
American–European opinion is mirrored in disagreements over
whether 'end use' or 'stated use' should be the standard applied to
potential Eastern bloc transfers. The debates surrounding these differences have intensified as high technology goods begin to supplant
manufactured items especially with respect to American and European
exports to the East.

The effectiveness of primarily American-backed controls within
COCOM has been questioned on essentially two grounds. The first is
the general availability of most sanctioned products from American
allies, resulting in harm, through loss of sales, essentially to only
American firms. This has been the reason for the continued American
efforts to legalize the extraterritorial application of sanctions to European firms in order to diminish the alternative availability of goods
from non-American producers.

The second difficulty in the American pursuit of export sanctions
concerns the ease with which trade secrets appear to find their way to
the East.[35] Pressure to minimize the application of restrictions on 'dual
use' goods thus emanates from European governments and often finds
favour with American firms and the United States Commerce Department. American firms lobbied, albeit unsuccessfully, for a proposed
1983 amendment to the Export Administration Act that would have
eliminated the need for export licences when the immediate purchaser

is a COCOM member.[36] The effect of that change would have been to negate the official United States position on 'end use' criteria for potential sales by allowing re-export with no limitations, a result strongly and successfully contested by the Defense Department and its Congressional allies.

The current Reagan administration's drive to limit, for essentially ideological reasons, the flow of sensitive technology to the East thus faces opposition from domestic exporters as well as risking non-compliance from European allies. Once again these states view American measures as politically motivated since the 1 per cent American share of East European sales ensures a minimal impact on its total market opportunities.[37] In turn any limits on the greater Western European market share in terms of sales opportunities severely diminishes its ability to maintain an efficient domestic industrial base and therefore ultimately the ability to compete on equal terms with American MNEs in global commercial competition. This is particularly true for West Germany, whose social ties and commercial contacts have substantially increased its share of East–West trade over the past few years. Notwithstanding the probability of increased intra-Alliance tensions the Reagan administration continues to pursue additional avenues to bring foreign partners within the ambit of American law and export-directed sanctions. Measures are pending which are designed to limit the transfer of processes in addition to existing restrictions on the export and re-export of goods.[38] In comparison, recent modifications to the Export Control Act are designed to make it easier to sell sought-after consumer goods, such as personal computers, transfers of which are virtually impossible to control in any case.[39] These modifications resulted in large measure from allied pressure within COCOM. In return for acceding to these European requests the United States now seeks to gain European cooperation in upgrading the ability effectively to implement measures against leaks in sales of more sensitive goods and processes. Both lessened restrictions and more efficient monitoring were the result of the 1985 export modifications detailed above, which established three stages of licensing procedures for mainly data processing products. Only in the third stage do restrictions overcome the presumption of saleability, thus allowing for more efficient control of such technological transfers to the East.

CORPORATE PARTNERS AND EXPORT OPPORTUNITIES

The management of export controls is made even more difficult by the centripetal tendency of Western firms when seeking partners to enhance their marketing and sales opportunities. A small pool of available high-technology firms ensures that European firms must pursue one of three options when seeking a partner: national groups, European consortia or arrangements with foreign, usually American, companies. Additionally the cooperative experiences of the past twenty years channel even these limited options so that cooperation with an American partner has become almost mandatory.

The previous chapter, detailing activities of American MNEs in the Community, underscored the inability of single European firms adequately to address global competition. Limited resources, narrowly defined markets and mixed levels of national assistance combined to mandate a response through cooperative arrangements. But regional groupings, with the possible exception of Airbus, generally floundered on the political underpinnings of these economically defined measures. Of greater importance though was the clear inability of European consortia to enter the United States sales market without an American partner. When combined with demonstrated American leadership in the marketing, if not the development, of relevant processes, European firms increasingly sought partners from the United States to enhance their sales opportunities. In so doing though the arrangement created one extra legal tie that could force the European partner to accept the extraterritorial application of American export sanctions or face exclusion from the benefits that were the original reason for such co-operation.

This outcome then places the process of European harmonization in direct tension with pragmatic business needs which are increasingly being required to compete on their own merits with less governmental intervention and direction. Although European consortia with Community funding, especially in the high-technology sectors, are being instituted to overcome the resource and marketing shortcomings of purely private ventures they are as yet inadequate to redress current competitive inequities. As the recent break-up of the European Fighter Aircraft consortium demonstrates traditional rivalries, especially in security products, still continue to diminish any incentives toward European cooperation.[40] While Community funding might offset resource scarcity caused by duplicative European efforts it cannot create the market opportunities offered through partnership with an American firm with access and ties to domestic purchasers. Thus the Community's challenge is not only to aggregate and enhance sales potential but also to create market opportunities through innovative measures designed to open the global market-place. One such success was the Community's role in the Tokyo Round of GATT that enabled the restrictive provisions of the Buy American Act to be limited with respect to commercial sales of civilian aircraft products.[41] As a result Airbus sales in the American market have increased dramatically since the implementation of that agreement.[42]

NOTES

1. 'The Decline of Europe', *Newsweek*, 8 April 1984, pp. 44–56.
2. 41 USC sections 10a–10c (1976).
3. 'Belgium Opts for U.S. F-16 Fighters over the French Mirage', *The Times*, 9 June 1975, p. 4.
4. Official Journal of the European Communities, *Communication for the Promotion of European Cooperation of European Conferences on Technology and Innovation*, 10 August 1984 (84/C210/82) no. C210/2; EC Commission, *The European Community and New Technologies*, August 1984 (Brussels: European File, 1984); EC Commission, *Discussion Paper on Improving the International Competitive Position of European Firms*, COM(83) 547, 14 September 1983.
5. European Parliament Working Document, *Report on European Armaments Procurement Cooperation*, 8 May 1978, Doc. 83/78, PE 50.944 (hereafter *The Klepsch Report*).
6. European Parliament Working Document, *Report on Arms Procurement within a Common Industrial Policy and Arms Sales*, 27 June 1983, Doc. 1-455/83 (hereafter *The Fergusson Report*), p 9.
7. European Parliament Working Document, *Report on Promoting Defence and Technology Cooperation among West European Countries*, December 1980, Doc. 1499/80 (hereafter *The Greenwood Report*).
8. *The Fergusson Report*, p. 10.
9. Ibid., pp. 10–11.
10. Ibid.
11. Ibid., p. 6.
12. Ibid., p. 17.
13. Ibid., p. 18.
14. Ibid., p. 21.
15. Ibid., p. 26.
16. Ibid.
17. European Parliament Working Document, *Opinion of the Committee on Economic and Monetary Affairs*, 18–19 January 1983, Doc. 1-455/83, p. 55.
18. Ibid., p. 54.
19. An excellent treatment of this topic may be found in 'High Tech Trade and National Security' in *Trade: U.S. Policy since 1945* (Washington, DC: Congressional Quarterly, Inc., 1984), pp. 199–214.
20. 'National Security and the Political Use of Trade Controls', *International Economic Relations*, John Jackson (St Paul, MN: West Publishing Co., 1977), pp. 941–78.
21. *Trade: U.S. Policy since 1945* (Washington, DC: Congressional Quarterly, Inc., 1984), pp. 199–209.
22. Homer Moyer and Linda Mabry, 'Export Controls as Instruments of Foreign Policy: The History, Legal Issues and Policy Lessons of Three Recent Cases', *Law and Policy in International Business*, 15, 1 (1983), pp. 1–173. European Parliament Working Document 1985–1986, *Report on Technology Transfer*, 30 September 1985, Doc. A2-99/85.
23. Beverly Crawford and Stefanie Lenway, 'Decision Modes and International

Regime Change: Western Collaboration on East–West Trade', *World Politics* (April 1985), pp. 375–403.
24. *Trade: U.S. Policy since 1945*, p. 204.
25. Moyer and Mabry, op. cit., p. 71.
26. Ibid., pp. 78–82.
27. Ibid., pp. 83–6.
28. 'US Approves the Sale of Oil Gear to Russians', *New York Times*, 7 March 1984, p. 25.
29. 'Computer Rule Shift', *New York Times*, 1 January 1985, p. 24.
30. *New York Times*, 15 March 1985, p. 29.
31. *Aviation Week and Space Technology*, 3 June 1985, p. 125.
32. Lynda Clarizio and Stephen Woolcock, 'American Weighs Export Controls: Security Versus Economic Interest', *The World Today* (March 1985), pp. 58–62.
33. *Strategic Survey 1983–1984* (London: IISS, 1984), pp. 19–23.
34. 'Spain Refuses to Sign Accord with United States on Controlling the Re-export of Technology', *El País* (Madrid), 8 May 1985, p. 15.
35. 'The East Bloc steps up its Industrial Espionage', *The German Tribune*, 26 May 1985, p. 1.
36. *Trade: U.S. Policy since 1945*, pp. 210–11.
37. Ibid., p. 206.
38. 'Industry Wary of Technology Transfer Bills', *Science*, 7 June 1985, pp. 1182–3.
39. 'Computer Rule Shift', *New York Times*, 1 January 1985, p. 24.
40. 'On a Wing and a Computer', *The Economist*, 10 August 1985, p. 34.
41. EC Commission, *The European Communities and the United States*, May 1982, 57/82 (Brussels: European Information, External Relations, 1982), pp. 5–11.
42. 'Europe's Airlines Raid the U.S.', *Time*, 24 September 1984, p. 61.

5 The coalescing of a European security policy

This study has now traced the environmental, perceptual and structural problems imposing themselves on the Community's ability to define a security policy. It remains now to discuss the factors and programmes that together might form the substance and structure of such an initiative.[1]

COMMUNITY FUNDING IN SUPPORT OF HIGH-TECHNOLOGY INDUSTRY

Financial arrangements are at the heart of the political and economic relationship that defines the Community. The CAP, British distress over negative monetary flows, Greek demands for $5 billion in agricultural supports and West German enthusiasm for the EMS, encapsulate what is a perennial topic underpinning the shape and scope of Community programmes and initiatives.

Community funding and central control of national resources in pursuit of regional objectives must of necessity flow from member agreement. Cautiously that sentiment has sought to direct available resources in pursuit of industrial programmes whose vitality will, to a great extent, determine the global position of the Community as a whole. The tension inherent in these pronouncements is essentially created by past practices which limit national ability to shift the focus of support from traditional to more innovative project areas. In this fashion Community financing must be viewed as an attempt to redirect existing fund allocations rather than merely to augment aid to existing or new recipients. The need to transfer the financing focus from traditional programmes in agriculture and manufacturing to high-technology and related areas is not only increasingly visible but also essential to future survival. The problem, as with most Community issues, is not new but that does not diminish its importance or centrality to current realignments.

Neither availability of resources nor Community neglect of this issue is the cause of Europe's inability to devise financial supports for its firms. It is generally acknowledged that Community and member funds directly available for research and indirectly provided through procurement preferences are 'in total roughly equal to those provided by the Community's major competitors'.[2] In a similar fashion the Commission has been developing financing proposals with great regularity and enthusiasm over the past fifteen years.[3] Neither demonstrated concern nor available resources though has been sufficient to overcome the essential and constant problem, the ability to exploit this potential through central, in sum Community, direction.

The framework for financial support measures is naturally the concept of European Monetary Union (EMU). Originally envisaged as a point along a unidirectional continuum from ECSC to political union, EMU has undergone revision to make it more conducive to the sectoral approach to integration now favoured within the Community. Thus while the EMS and its attendant currency, the ECU, can find their antecedents in EMU, their implementation has been successful only because of a demonstrated willingness to forgo the optimal solution in the face of short-term political constraints. While important, the EMS and the ECU merely establish the framework and the means for financial support, but neither supplies the specific programmes designed to pursue these agreed objectives. Indeed it has been these specific programmes seeking to augment Community responsibility at the expense of member control that have been at the heart of the political and economic bargaining in the area of financial supports for Community firms. Prior to discussing current Community financial measures it is instructive to review briefly past suggestions which, for the most part, have been rejected or remain moribund for their content and for insights on what must now be done differently.

Past proposals for Community export assistance

Broadly addressed under the heading of a Community export policy, numerous measures were proposed by the Commission to redress the competitive inadequacies created by a financial support system fragmented along national lines. The Commission's desire to pursue these measures stemmed from two fundamental concerns. Foremost was the desire of members to continue support to national firms even though in 'opposition to the spirit of the Rome Treaty and . . . difficult to reconcile with the implementation of an effective Community commercial policy'.[4] Second was the existence of unified financing arrangements in the United States grouped around a single currency and loosely administered by the Export-Import Bank (EXIM), which generated advantages to American firms in global markets.[5] Since the Com-

munity's primary role in developing a common export policy was
established by Article 114 of the Treaty of Rome, the Commission
began to initiate proposals to support the international positioning of
its firms. Although proposals such as the European Company (SE)
were part of these initiatives, specific financing measures are even more
crucial to this inquiry.[6] In this latter group are two of particular
importance, the European Export Bank and European Development
Contracts.

The 1976 European Export Bank (EEB) proposal was a Community
instrument designed to act as sole source financing for European firms
in their efforts to develop an international competitive position in
pursuit of foreign market opportunities.[7] The European Investment
Bank (EIB), designed to meet intra-Community financing needs and
subject to direct member control, was not viewed as appropriate since
the EEB's secondary function was to promote the unification of
member export policies and programmes.[8] Quite simply, the EEB was
designed to substitute a single Community export assistance programme in place of separate national support measures. The EEB
would initially be financed by capital of 100 million UA from the
central budget and later through loans guaranteed by the Community.
EEB operations were viewed as complementary to member financial
institutions only until unification under Community auspices could be
accomplished. In light of the 1972 Paris Summit declaration of
'political union of 1980', this objective was not without support or
validity.

Support for the EEB was strong and included endorsements from
member financial and industrial circles as well as from the European
Parliament and Commission. Consistent with this support, funding for
the EEB was included by the Commission in its annual budgets even
though official approval by the Council of Ministers was still pending.
Ultimately the EEB proposal was never passed by the Council. Its dual
role of consortium financing and stimulus to unification of member
export programmes was narrowed with the elimination of the latter
and the subordination of the former by requiring that the EEB become
a department of the EIB. The actual proposal for an independent EEB
was officially dropped from Council consideration in July 1980.[9]

The second of these early Commission proposals to assist Community export industries, especially those active in high-technology
sectors, was the proposal on Community Development Contracts
(CDC).[10] CDCs were to be offered to consortia of Community firms
which sought to increase their competitive capabilities in advanced
technology areas. CDCs were viewed as complementary to the directive
on public contracts by specifically rewarding those firms planning in

regional rather than in national terms. By undermining the dependence of Community firms on national assistance the Commission assumed that these measures would create the single industrial market required to compete with American MNEs. Priority for such assistance would be accorded to firms 'which have decided to engage in transnational cooperation and restructuring'.[11] Major beneficiaries were to be high-technology firms which were subject to intense competition from foreign MNEs and whose potential as a result remained latent. Small and medium-sized firms as well as large enterprises could be eligible for such assistance.[12]

EDCs became a cornerstone in all Commission programmes to merge European capability to meet foreign competition. The 1976 *Informatics Study*, the precursor of the Esprit project, expressly endorsed their use and importance to the high-technology sectors.[13] As with the EEB, the EDC was never formally enacted, although parts of both proposals were later incorporated by subsequent financing initiatives.

Current measures and lessons learned

The need for programmes such as the EEB and EDC remains and has assumed increased importance because of the continued inability of Community firms in export-orientated high-technology markets. The attraction of the ECU in commercial use attests to the desirability of a single currency for trade, even though the EMS does not carry the latent political content that full implementation of the EMU would have.[14] The merging of members' financial resources has to a great extent been carried out within the Esprit, again attesting to the economic wisdom of the preceding Commission efforts. In the more narrow area of export financing three related lessons may be gleaned from these early Commission efforts. First is the need to coordinate the discrete sources of support in·pursuit of a regional capability. Second, and as important, is the need to direct this support toward small and medium-sized firms whose activities in innovations research involve risk and are thus generally incapable of attracting investment capital from more traditional sources. Finally is the need to concentrate these funds on high-technology research and implementation in pursuit of comprehensive regional objectives. The current Commission financing proposals have taken these three lessons to heart and have produced a new financing package designed to meet the economic objectives of EEB and EDC, while muting the political overtones that caused the failure of the earlier proposals.

The new vehicle to attain a Community financing objective is the European Innovation Loan (EIL).[15] Proposed in 1983, the EIL is designed to do many of the same things as earlier proposals and essentially to 'fund . . . innovative projects in sectors which introduce new products, devise new processes or apply innovatory technologies'.[16] Initially funded at 100 million ECU, very similar to the level for the original EEB, loans would be made to small and medium-sized firms whose inability to attract venture capital has resulted in a lack of risk-taking when compared to the results of the American market. To increase available funding and to ensure member participation, each Community grant would be matched by a 'financial intermediary', generally a bank, or could be given directly to that entity which would in turn dispense funds to eligible firms.[17] The EIL is specifically designed to redress the continued fragmentation of the Community's internal market, an objective identical to that of the EDC. Finally, there is provision in the proposal to create a specialized financial institution tentatively called the European Financial Agency whose sole responsibility would be to monitor and dispense resources in accord with Community planning objectives.[18] While the future of the EIL is uncertain, its initiation as a response to a direct call by the European Council suggests that it will fare better than the previously Commission-directed EEB and EDC, although owing much of its success to the groundwork laid by these failed initiatives.

COMMUNITY PROGRAMMES IN DATA PROCESSING AND ALLIED AREAS

The inability of the Community to realize its goal of a comprehensive data processing capability by 1980 did not lessen the need for such a programme. Innovations technology (IT), incuding data processing, is acknowledged to be the fastest growing global industry, with an estimated turn over of $500 billion by 1990 (at 1980 prices). Two-thirds of the Community's GNP is influenced by these technologies which also directly or indirectly account for 50 per cent of civilian employment in Europe.[19] The ability of the Community's industries to compete in this sector is a matter of survival, a capability that has deteriorated over the past decade. Community data processing and allied technologies, while still impressive, are increasingly clustered in older products destined either for replacement parts or for less demanding Third World markets.

To meet Community requirements, European firms too often have to depend on imported technologies or on licensing from abroad.[20] Thus the IT sector, like few other industrial sectors, is essential to and indicative of the Community's ability to maintain its role as a leading service economy comparable to those of the United States and Japan.

'The EC spends more than two times as much as Japan on research. But industrial application falls behind.'[21] A great deal of the blame for the faltering Community role in ITs may be traced to its inability to follow through on the proposals contained in the 1976 *Informatics Study*. Conversely, it is the coincidence of past failures and the continued deterioration of the Community's present global competitive position that has lent a sense of urgency, including a new-found willingness to compromise on current initiatives.

Although the 1976 *Informatics Study* floundered because of its comprehensive scope, it also fell foul of the perennial Community problem of national versus central direction. Between 1977 and 1979, new or existing national programmes in the United Kingdom, France, West Germany and Italy targeted approximately 360 million ECU to assist national ventures.[22] But national direction, no matter how well thought out, was and continued to be incapable of solving the two major obstacles facing Community high technology firms: lack of planning coordination and resource fragmentation. State assistance sought to maintain the competitiveness of national companies in their domestic markets essentially by local cooperation or through licensing agreements primarily with American MNEs. The outcome of this response is that the Community still imports 80 per cent of its integrated circuits while the United States and Japan remain net exporters.[23] The situation in all other aspects of IT production reflects a similar European decline relative to the United States and Japan and replicates the market situation that existed in the mid-1970s and which prompted the original 1976 programme on informatics. Much of the American dominance is due to defence-related spending, which accounted for 49 per cent of total American research and development in 1982.[24] Additionally, commercial application of defence spin-offs continues as a major indirect source of American government assistance to industry. The industrial limitations created by the absence of a similar Community defence research and development capability are further intensified by the continued existence of separate national programmes designed to assist only domestic firms. It has long been the position of the Commission and the Parliament that, at a minimum, members' civilian research and development resources should be coordinated in some fashion. The stumbling block has been at the national governmental and industrial levels which have held that economic assets must remain firmly wedded to member direction and control. In this way, cooperation with American MNEs has been preferred to increased European coordination because of the lack of a political commitment exemplified by these external ties. A change of direction has only recently been prompted by the recognition that American and Community economic objectives are diverging, thus creating substantial support for new Community-derived initiatives.

Corporate support for a new Community initiative was sparked in 1983 when representatives of the major European IT firms wrote to Commission Vice President Davignon, then Commissioner for Industry, and stated that 'unless a cooperative industrial programme of a sufficient magnitude can be mounted, most if not all of the current IT industry [would] disappear in a few years time'.[25] On 11 September 1979, the Council of Ministers had already adopted a resolution on this topic which stated that the Community had a twofold responsibility to 'fill the gaps in national programmes' and also to concentrate on the resources essential to allow European firms to meet global competition in advanced technology products by 1985.[26] This overt acknowledgement of a need for structural reorientation now merged with national sentiments in support of Community leadership in what has come to be termed the Esprit project.

Esprit: the search for a European IT capability

The pilot stage of the European Strategic Programme for Research and Development in Innovation Technologies (Esprit) began at the end of 1982 and served initially to link 200 research programmes within 638 businesses and universities in all ten Community members around a core of fifteen projects.[27] The full-scale Esprit programme began in 1984 and is scheduled to last for ten years, with a total budget of 1,500 million ECU for the first half of that initial period (1 ECU = US$0.87 on 8 March 1984). The Commission and national governments are each to provide 50 per cent of Esprit financing. The programme, a result of coordination between universities, firms and national governments, is designed 'to lay the foundations for a fully competitive European industry in the next decade'.[28] To realize this objective there are five fields of emphasis, three of which address basic development of high-technology capabilities while the remaining two focus on the application of results to the needs of the market-place. Within these five fields projects will be chosen by the Community from applications submitted by EC-based firms and institutions which, with minor exceptions, must involve more than one member state. A key to Esprit projects is the requirement that research results be distributed to all interested parties, a requirement that is central to the creation of a shared pool of research and development information. Additionally this requirement moves the Community toward the secondary aid procedures for government contracts now successfully utilized in the American system of national aid to technologically orientated companies. Among the projects funded in 1983 were those sponsored by Siemens and Standard Telecom Laboratories, each heading consortia of Community firms engaged in various aspects of IT research.[29] Separate national programmes, where they still exist, are brought into the Esprit system by a requirement to consult and inform on all projects that members are funding or otherwise engaged in.[30] Dissemination of project results is achieved through various agencies including CAVE workshops where all members are invited to send observers. To ensure the timely commercial application of research, contractors are required to publish findings as well as to exploit commercially results within one year or to make them available to others within the Community for their use.[31]

The cooperation exemplified by Esprit has already been transferred to other areas. Recently six European computer manufacturers announced an agreement to standardize their software operating system based on the UNIX system developed by AT&T.[32] This goes a long way towards ending the basic issue of language compatibility that plagued these same firms in the 1970s. The incompatibility of UNIX with IBM machines also creates new market opportunities by offering a proven alternative supplier to that American MNE. Although IBM is toying with a programme that would adapt UNIX to its own products this still does not detract from what is a major step towards a co-ordinated Community response to the IT issue.

Problems and prospects for Esprit

Any assessment of the year-old Esprit programme and its allied IT initiatives must of necessity be based on prescience rather than on an established track record. Nevertheless, four potential problem areas stand out. Foremost are past failures to achieve essentially these same objectives. Limited resources and a lack of clear commitment at member-government level doomed the more comprehensive 1976 programme and even more limited cooperative ventures such as Unidata. The Esprit programme acknowledged these past failures by limiting its proposals and by ensuring member and Community support at an early stage throughout the administrative and financial thrust of its projects. Of equal importance is the recognition often articulated but only recently accepted that Europe can no longer depend on United States largess to sustain its global economic aspirations. Cooperation in pursuit of both regional and national objectives is no longer only a desirable goal but is rather a matter of survival. This necessity of co-ordinated action in pursuit of a Community presence and identity in ITs is the second problem area. Its current manifestation is over the manner best suited to responding to the American offer of access to the research and development aspects of SDI with its obvious commercial applications for military and civilian products. The global dominance of many American firms has been founded on this concept of dual use products. Applications are due in large measure to the requirements of the defence sector, which has shown itself to be a versatile and creative utilizer of the latest innovations. Defence requirements then provide the civilian market with ready-made and fully paid-for innovations merely seeking new uses. Since Esprit is strictly orientated towards the non-defence market it will continue, by necessity, to duplicate national defence research efforts with little possibility of cross-over applications. The necessity for some Community capability to merge commercial and military projects, although extremely sensitive, is increasingly mandated by events. Finally, there remains the spectre of IBM. Still the dominant force in Europe, there is a question of whether the limited scope of Esprit will enable Community firms to do more than nibble on the edges of competition. Additionally IBM has long argued that it should be considered a Community firm, given its high content of regionally produced parts and large number of local employees.[33] While seductive in its reasoning, acceptance of IBM's position would effectively end any hopes Community firms might have of a global competitive position via the instrument of Esprit.

ARMS PRODUCTION COOPERATION AND A EUROPEAN SECURITY POLICY

It is naïve to suggest that the economic efficiencies attainable through aggregation of European arms production capabilities are sufficient to overcome the political reality of control over industrial assets integral to a state's security policy. The disappearance of the 1975 Community Aerospace Programme and the later Klepsch proposal on procurement cooperation attest to the deeply held belief that overt security matters must remain the province of the state. In addition to this concept of stature are the added factors of jobs, revenue and foreign policy leverage. Consortia such as that working on the Tornado project are acceptable essentially because national control over production and sales is neither diminished nor limited by such cooperation.

Yet recurring examples of waste and duplication in pursuit of national security assets continue to surface to keep the debate over regional planning alive. Most recently discussion has centred on the negotiations to build the European Fighter Aircraft (EFA) as a replacement for current West German, Spanish and British aircraft and to provide an export alternative to new designs from the United States.[34] In addition to its military role the EFA was seen as an all-European venture to enhance regional industrial and technological capabilities as well as to diminish the incentive to join as a subcontractor to parallel American aircraft developments. This latter aspect was a direct response to the subcontractor role assumed in the mid-1970s by several European NATO states on the American F-16 project.[35] As one British aerospace executive stated: 'This time we want, and will get, the entire handle on the project.'[36]

Regional production of the EFA would enable two other security-related issues to be addressed in a fashion conducive to European planning objectives. First is the continuing inequity in the NATO 'two-way' street, which stands at an 8:1 disadvantage in military sales for a total European annual deficit nearing $2 billion.[37] The military advantage of a single system adopted by European NATO members would allow increased political leverage to be brought to bear in favour of American purchases of that aircraft. The second advantage accruing from the EFA would be in the export market. Aside from the revenues generated a European aircraft would not be subject to the export controls associated with partnership on an American project.[38] In this manner the EFA could garner sales that are prohibited to American MNEs because of foreign-policy-related export controls. When intra-European, intra-NATO and export sales are totalled the potential economic success of the EFA should serve to overcome any nationally derived obstacles to its implementation.

Once again though a well-positioned, Europe-orientated initiative has gone off the rails. On 2 August 1985, the five-member EFA consortium disbanded because of an inability to agree on the purpose, design and thus the division of labour associated with the project. Britain, West Germany and Italy have since agreed to cooperate on a large fighter that will also have a ground attack role, while France will build a smaller and cheaper aircraft designed primarily for ground attack. The other consortium member, Spain, has recently purchased 72 American F-18 Hornets, but might still work as a subcontractor on the French venture.[39]

The ramifications of these decisions are substantial and negatively affect each of the benefits that a true European fighter would have provided. Sales of the Tornado have been limited to its consortium members, Britain, West Germany and Italy, strongly suggesting that the export potential of their new fighter venture might also be minimal. The political leverage to readjust intra-NATO sales will similarly disappear, leaving any American alternative aircraft the probable beneficiary of non-consortium purchasers. Once again European design innovations capable of sustaining acceptable sales levels are derailed by squabbling over project leadership, a situation that will redound to the benefit of American aircraft firms. Finally, given the mission overlap between the two alternative European ventures, it is to be expected that they will compete against each other for potential markets, further diminishing the opportunity to rationalize regional production, industrial, and technological capabilities.

The adoption of Klepsch's EAPA would greatly ease the factors that lead to this divisive solution on the EFA project. The neglect of that proposal within Community policy circles strongly suggests the level of support remaining for its short-term adoption. Yet its prescriptions, rational and objectives remain sound and reflective of sentiment held within member governments and industrial circles. Perhaps, then, what has doomed the proposal is its singularity and remoteness from more prosaic and thus more acceptable regional cooperative ventures. To offset that singularity, EFA-type projects must be included among the several high-technology ventures where the sharing of research and development, design and marketing can serve to diminish the defence aspects of the project, thereby removing one further nationally derived obstacle to regional security cooperation.

SPACE PROGRAMMES AND THE STRATEGIC DEFENSE INITIATIVE (SDI)

The lure of space has long been associated with competing visions of space battles, alien life forms and new frontiers for joint exploration by the peoples of earth. This duality was reinforced by the first Sputnik launch which was heralded as a scientific and engineering achievement but which gave rise to the present central defence role of the ICBM. So, too, current initiatives combine, in varying degrees, images from the competing if increasingly overlapping worlds of commerce and combat. Central to these images is the spectre of losing the initiative in research and development, innovations and derivative technologies essential to any space-based presence.

The 'dual use' of many of these projects has allowed an ancillary Community role gradually to be expanded to the point where a European space-based presence is no longer out of the realm of at least the planning stage.[40] The two programmes currently under discussion in the Alliance are those of a primarily commercial shuttle/base and the essentially military Strategic Defense Initiative (SDI). Derivatives from these major programmes include projects such as drug production, navigation aids and resource and mineral mapping. While the Soviet Union's interest in these concerns is without question it is the role of these Alliance initiatives in an evolving European security policy around which controversy has coalesced.

The Strategic Defense Initiative and European Security Policy

The SDI was unveiled by President Reagan in March 1983 as a research programme designed to pursue new technologies that might assist in the defence of the United States and its allies from ballistic missile attack. Revolutionary in its defence implications, moving from avenging an attack to negating one, SDI sought to capitalize on developments in new technologies such as lasers where progress had made military application of pure research feasible. Although fundamental questions on financing and system effectiveness remain, the short-term debate centres on the SDI's role in intra-Alliance political and economic relations.[41] While the SDI's role in the defence of the United States is clear, its role in the extended deterrence guarantees that are incorporated under the American 'nuclear umbrella' is less precise. Although it is clear that NATO and Western Europe would be prime candidates for new guarantees, it is uncertain whether these are feasible or, if feasible, whether they will be credible. What, for example, might be the relationship between SDI and the current NATO doctrine of 'first use'? What impact does SDI have on the intermediate nuclear balance affected between the SS-20 and the Pershing II? Would the proposed inviolability of the American homeland increase or decrease the likelihood of war, at whatever level, in Western Europe.

Europe's response to the programme has been mixed and reflects a desire to ensure its security arrangements but not at the expense of military and technological deference to the United States. Possession of even a basic SDI system by the United States would downgrade the foreign policy options now garnered by Britain and France because of possession of their own strategic systems. Simultaneously, lack of access to the innovations now being developed in support of the SDI would be another obstacle in Europe's effort to achieve competitive stature against the United States and Japan in future technologies and their commercial uses. Fearing a countermove by the Soviet Union, either through development of a similar capability or by significant expansion of their existing strategic arsenal, the French government has strongly criticized the SDI programme essentially because it would signal the erosion of France's own deterrent systems and with it France's global political stature.[42] Although originally supportive of the SDI proposal, the Kohl government, partially in response to fervent domestic opposition, has become more critical of the project and its repercussions on the independence of West German foreign policy.[43]

Although the United Kingdom has expressed support for the project, that position is inextricably linked to the presence of Prime Minister Thatcher whose stature and indeed office is likely to be severely challenged in coming national elections.

Although European responses to the SDI are national in origin, it is in President Reagan's attempts to garner Allied political support for the venture that a Community role emerges. The sweetener offered to induce European political support of the SDI is a sharing of the economic and technological contracts associated with the project. This means direct access to research, which might then be translated into profitable commercial ventures by European firms participating in the programme.[44] It is in the translation process that the Community's role emerges. To utilize these shared technologies effectively requires a research and development and industrial effort beyond the capability of any single European state. It is only in the coordination of national assets that the benefits of derivative technologies may emerge and be utilized to benefit European firms and their futures. Consortia of national firms may be developed to exclude or minimize Community involvement. But events surrounding the record of space-related initiatives strongly suggest support for Community leadership in the commercial and perhaps even in the future defence implications of the effort. Space-related activities will at some time be included on the arms control agenda of the superpowers. To ensure responsiveness to European goals in space requires the presence of an entity that can bargain as an equal with the United States and the Soviet Union. The position of the Community as the only entity with that potential power strongly supports its inclusion and active participation in these initial responses to the American offer. The recent French suggestion which proposed 'an intimate French–German technological union with the addition of other interested European states' is an effort to create a new bargain, to replace the outdated CAP, which might then form the basis of that Community role in space.[45]

While the European attraction to the SDI has gradually shifted from the military to the economic sphere, the potential for direct Community involvement has not been so clearly manifested. A partial reason may be suggested by the American preference for European participation on a bilateral basis at either governmental or private levels rather than a coordinated regional response.[46] A more persuasive reason derives from the absence of national, let alone regional, policy on how best to respond to Secretary of Defense Weinberger's March 1985 offer for a European role in the SDI.[47] While European defence ministers are generally united in favour of participation, foreign ministers are less sanguine about the ramifications of such an affirmative response. Their concern derives from the desire to ensure political control and timing of such participation, an objective which they fear might evaporate if European firms become too closely linked with and supportive of the American effort. To ensure a politically palatable arrangement with sufficient controls to meet domestic concerns yet with enough leeway to derive the economic benefits of joint European–American action has been a heated topic of debate. Prodded by the reluctance of France to support the deterioration of its deterrent force and the political inability of West Germany to endorse openly such a sensitive issue, a European response now appears to be emerging within the parameters of the Eureka project.[48]

Eureka was proposed by President Mitterrand as a means of pursuing the technological innovations and civilian applications of SDI research without the defence overtones of a direct role in the security aspects of the project. Cognisant of the advances in commercial products derived from the partnership between NASA and the American Defense Department, France and other European states are determined not to widen further the existing technological gap by inaction or by allowing their available resources to be so tied to the American effort as to negate any coordinated European response. Eureka, although nationally derived, is clearly a precursor of joint European responsibility for the initiative and, more importantly, a long-term instrument to control and channel future commercial application of derived technologies. Increasingly Eureka is viewed as a parallel rather than an alternative to participation in SDI, making it even easier to direct the effort within the Community industrial policy with little chance of taint and thus opposition because of direct military ramifications.[49]

An institutional framework is required to focus this joint effort and to mesh that response into other coordinated European projects. Although the defence implications of the SDI have suggested that the European response be formulated within the WEU, this will be a short-lived phenomenon. To continue to isolate defence from political and economic matters is to maintain the artificial division of sovereignty that dates from the demise of the EDC in 1954. Cooperation is a political determinate and, when based on increasingly economic arguments, strongly suggests that the Community is the institution which must ultimately secure responsibility for this project.[50] It is a reasonable adjunct to high-technology initiatives within the industrial policy as well as an obvious parallel and companion to ongoing and successful commercial initiatives in the area of space.

The commercial use of space: the European Space Agency (ESA)

European cooperation for the commercial exploitation of space began more than twenty-five years ago when the Preparatory Commission for European Space Research (COPERS) was established on 1 December 1960.[51] COPERS included the major Community members as well as neutral states such as Austria, Sweden and Switzerland. COPERS was given the task of reviewing existing space activities in Europe and, within one year, of drafting a development programme to establish a European space organization capable of implementing that initiative. The report that was issued envisaged a programme to develop and launch 440 rockets and thirty-four satellites at a total cost of approximately $421 million.[52]

As a result of that programme review the European Space Research Organization (ESRO) was formed in June 1962, with ten of the original COPERS members joining this new organization. After protracted negotiations ESRO's mission was defined as the development and utilization of satellites for commercial purposes. Concurrently, and based on British instigation, was the formation of the European Launcher Development Organization (ELDO) in April 1962 and dedicated to the pursuit of a European launch vehicle. Although sharing complementary memberships ESRO and ELDO remained quite separate and much of the history of European space initiatives revolves about the conflict between these two organizations.[53] They did serve to articulate a common European position and thus more favourable entry terms on commercial projects such as Intelsat as well as on several NASA-originated missions. The friction between ESRO and ELDO was finally terminated with the creation of the European Space Agency (ESA) in 1975 designed to merge separate national efforts into a European whole.

The current European organization for cooperation in space has become the eleven-member European Space Agency, designed to explore the peaceful and commercial uses of space. The ESA's membership includes most Community members, with the notable exception of Greece and Portugal. Its budget is provided by mandatory levels from each member on designated joint projects plus additional moneys earmarked for specific projects such as Spacelab. Since 1975 ESA has spent more than $6 billion on joint projects, with separate national ventures contributing even more to the total.[54]

While the ESA is a cooperative European effort, its majority members are France, West Germany, Italy and Britain. The French contribution remains the largest essentially because of its control over Arianespace which provides the launch vehicles for ESA flights. The

government–firm relationship is especially strong within ESA,
although the French situation, where one individual heads both the
French Space Agency and the commercial aspects of Ariane applications, is somewhat atypical. France has also taken the lead in
championing the development of a small space shuttle, the Hermes, to
provide a European counter to the American venture. The contributions of West Germany and Italy, aside from funding, are centred on
the development of the Columbus, an updated module designed to be
compatible with an American space station and designed to house
individuals and equipment for extended stays in space in support of
commercial projects.[55]

Although ESA projects and expenditures pale beside NASA's efforts
and plans, the consortium remains an unqualified success. James
Beggs, NASA Administrator, told a 1985 Congressional hearing: 'All I
can tell you is that our position in the market has deteriorated in the
past year. In the past 14 months in the commercial launch area, we
won five and they [Western Europe] won five and nobody else won
any.'[56] ESA's success may be attributed to several factors. Key among
them are reliability and cost. Passage on the American space shuttle
costs about $38 million, while on an ESA flight the cost is between $25
and $30 million. Although less versatile than the shuttle, Ariane
launchers are able to put payloads directly into the preferred position
of a geosynchronous stationary orbit. Additionally, Arianespace, representing a consortium of European firms, banks and national agencies,
provides attractive financing and support to prospective customers.
This tight government support for Arianespace was recently illustrated
by the complaint filed against it alleging violation of Section 201 of the
United States Trade Act on the basis of unfair pricing arrangements
designed illegally to undercut American firms active in the commercial
use of space.[57] The ESA position is strongest particularly when addressing the limited space requirements of Third World clients. In April
1985 the first Arab satellite was successfully launched by the ESA,
capitalizing on Third World desires to seek alternatives to cooperation
with either superpower. Finally, there is the commitment of members
to support and expand ESA's scope of operations. In January 1985 the
first ministerial meeting of the ESA since 1977 convened to guide institutional goals between several attractive options. The speed of agreement and the clarity of objectives was a direct outgrowth of member
support for both the ESA and its use in commercially exploiting space
opportunities. At that meeting:

(1) $2.1 billion was earmarked to develop an Ariane 5 launcher that
    will increase more than three times the present payload of
    15 metric tons;

(2) it was agreed to accept the American invitation to participate in the $10 billion permanent space station to be launched in the early 1990s;

(3) $2 billion was voted to fund Columbus as an independent part of a space station that could be detached to form the basis of an independent European space station.[58]

The obvious question that must be raised is why such a rare area of member high-technology cooperation continues to remain separate from the Community and its related industrial initiatives. One suggestion is raised by Roy Gibson, ex-Director General of the ESA, who noted that the Commission was never really intrigued 'by ESA or by space affairs in general', even though some officials from both organizations maintained informal but regular contacts over the years.[59]

A more likely suggestion is the desire by leading ESA members, in particular France, to retain programme control in order to ensure an organizational agenda consistent with national objectives. Indeed the only manifest sector of Community–ESA overlap is in the area of remote sensing for agricultural, resource and pollution mapping where an EC programme has allocated 18.35 million ECU and ninety-seven staff members to the project.[60] The probability of closer Community–ESA relations, notwithstanding a tradition of separation, is extremely good when one considers the coincidence of the Esprit and Eureka initiatives with ESA-projected short-term projects. While not minimizing the military potential of a space shuttle, the commercial applications of ESA–Community projects strongly suggests their merger as long as member objectives within the former would be assured of protection in any new institutional alignment of roles and responsibilities.

EUROPEAN MULTINATIONALS AND A COMMUNITY SECURITY POLICY

MNEs have become the major instrument by which states implement the mechanics of current and proposed security policies. The demise of the perspective that MNEs would become independent policy-making actors equal or superior to the state has ensured their attention to working through the prevailing international economic system grounded on state power.[61] This attitude is enhanced by state control of companies in Europe or by the close government–firms defence contacts found in the United States. This is not to gainsay corporate efforts to influence national objectives but rather to underscore their acknowledgement of the primacy of the state in international commercial and security matters. But clearly the international experience of corporations remains a major source of influence to be successfully exploited where national objectives remain unformed or where clashes between states create a commercial opportunity. The technical requisites and lack of identity beween American and European commercial and security objectives enhance the opportunity for MNE action. This latitude exists primarily because of MNE's near monopoly over the means to effect national policy for security production. Profits, contacts and derivative commercial applications ensure keen competition between these firms for government largess and account for the different development patterns that security-active MNEs have progressed through. Their greater dependence on national contracts and subsidies ensures that their sensitivity to government direction will be greater than for more commercially directed firms such as IBM. The negative implications of this security interaction between firms and state are that the government often has nowhere else to turn when dissatisfied with the contractual bargain for a product. The inability of the United States government significantly to alter the price charged for the Trident submarine by Electric Boat is but one outcome of this dependent relationship. The situation in Europe is somewhat different since most security-active firms are nationalized or otherwise dependent on state assistance and therefore more receptive to government direction. Even so, the problems inherent in an industrial structure of single producers exist, although in differing degrees, for both Europe and the United States. Thus the role of the European MNE in the development of a regional security policy is multi-faceted. Aggregation of corporate assets and resources does not automatically ensure that production and policy direction will be supportive of regional objectives if firms continue to remain dependent on national direction and assistance. How to break the symbiosis of state–firm contacts in pursuit of Community-directed programmes then emerges as the key to progress and the question for resolution.[62]

The Community's overall approach toward defining a regional MNE policy may be said to have anticipated three stages of development.[63] The initial step was the removal of obstacles to the free movement of goods, services and capital throughout the region. These original goals of the Treaty of Rome were implemented indirectly through the adoption of the EMS in 1979 and more directly through various directives and regulations on corporate operating practices. Although measures such as those on public procurement policy continue to be subject to debate by and large full implementation is being delayed essentially to allow time for compensating bargains to ease ultimate member compliance. The second stage of the Community's MNE policy framework builds directly on the success of these initial efforts by substituting a harmonized legal framework in place of diverse and often competing national structures. This ability springs mainly from the legal obligations of Article 100 which require that members harmonize laws in sectors directly within the Community's policy-making ambit. Harmonization does not require the unification of member systems under Community control, instead allowing the continuation of national direction in support of regionally defined objectives. This is the reason why the Directive rather than the Regulation, which does require ceding of control to the region, has become the preferred instrument of Community initiatives. In this fashion members may continue to control directly their security-active firms since the scope of harmonization efforts does not include military or defence production. Even when a firm is involved in 'dual use' production, harmonization simply requires that operating practices, such as accounting measures, conform to the regional standard.

It is the final stage of regional control over MNE activities within Community sectors of action which has proved the most elusive. Although a neutral legal instrument, the use of the Directive to the clear exclusion of the Regulation reflects the politically sensitive nature of the underlying economic control objective that is actually being pursued. Earlier efforts such as the EEB and the EDC, both phrased as Regulations, floundered on the lack of willingness among members to cede control over vital economic and industrial assets. This member reticence is exacerbated when target firms and sectors are also vital to security production with its corollary implications for domestic employment, export sales and foreign policy independence. Thus competition between regional and national direction of corporate capability continues, most recently illustrated in the ambivalence over how best to respond to the American offer of subcontractor or partnership status in the research and development phase of the SDI. While the economic benefits flowing from a European role in that venture are apparent, it is in the member–Community debate over programme control that progress has slowed.

Clearly the question for the Community is the nature of the inducements it can offer members and firms to persuade them to loosen state-centred ties in pursuit of both regional and international economic opportunities. Cooperative ventures in Europe have a long history, with varying roles envisaged or devised for the Community. Two such ventures are the consortia to produce the Airbus and the Tornado. The Community role in Airbus has been an indirect one, essentially providing access in international forums to enhance export sales for what still remains a member-directed consortium. Because of the defence role of the Tornado there was no direct Community role in that venture and none is now anticipated for its follow-on project, the European

Fighter Aircraft. Although both Airbus and Tornado appear equally successful in terms of sales and national cooperation, each gives rise to very different long-term implications and lessons for regional security activity.

The Tornado, or, as it was originally titled, the Multi-Role Combat Aircraft (MRCA), was designed to fulfil a multiplicity of combat roles within the demands of a European warfare scenario. Although criticized by Air Force officers as inadequate to its missions, essentially because of this flexibility, the Tornado is still held up as an example of what European cooperation can accomplish to support regional objectives and to lessen dependence on American products within the NATO sales environment.[64] Tornado supporters point to the 'Europeanness' of the aircraft, especially when contrasted with the subcontractor role of several European NATO members on the co-production of the American F-16 fighter. Detractors note that the price for this cooperation was so high, both in monetary terms and in product usefulness, as to render any such future agreements prohibitive. In particular the Tornado was to be offered as a European export alternative to American aircraft. While global demand for American planes such as the F-15 and F-16 remains high, sales of the Tornado have been limited solely to members of the production consortium.

Airbus products were also designed as alternatives to American aircraft from Boeing and McDonnell Douglas. But, unlike the Tornado consortium, Airbus utilized Community assistance to break down entry barriers to foreign markets, resulting in a situation where sales have increased in all export sectors but particularly in the American market. It is in this concept of international 'access' that the Community's opportunity to induce member acquiescence to its MNE policy emerges.

The management of access may be broken into two dimensions. Internally Community aggregation of MNE assets is inducible by the panoply of financial, marketing and legal incentives produced by regional agreement and directed toward enhancing competitive capability in global commercial markets. In this fashion the ability of the Community to certify a consortium as regionally directed eliminates the potential anti-trust prosecution of corporate operations that competitors such as IBM have faced in the past. Other inducements have been the subject of previous sections in this chapter.

The second dimension of access exists at international levels and is the area where Community participation emerges as unique in its policy implications. This mediating role between internal and external actors is also suggested by the requirements of complex interdependence. The ability of the Commission to speak for a regional industrial capability, so effectively demonstrated in support of Airbus in 1979 at the Tokyo Round of GATT, enables it to also have a major influence on agenda formation at these levels. A direct Community involvement in international negotiations would also enhance regional positions because of the ability to practice issue linkage. Discreteness in American–European negotiations on agriculture, trade and technological cooperation could, as a result, be eliminated. The existence of a Community stance supported by traditionally greater government–firm interaction would support the European position against often competing American commercial actors. Finally, the experience of the Commission in manœuvring between competing state and regional actors would be magnified at international levels. A derivative effect might be support for the Commission from American participants who are often frustrated by the welter of institutions, organizations and actors that must be consulted when contemplating a corporate position or official policy initiative towards or within Europe.

That external mediating role is ultimately dependent on the existence of an internal arrangement sympathetic to the emergence of a Community security policy. The shape and scope of that internal structure must acknowledge a leading, if not primary, role for the Community over the direction which regional harmonization must pursue. The inability to implement a regional aerospace policy in 1975 contrasts to the success of a member-regional mix in Esprit and Airbus to establish the parameters within which that Community involvement may be developed.

THE NEW BARGAIN: A EUROPEAN TECHNOLOGY POLICY (ETP)

The need for a European security policy has again assumed a position of agenda dominance partially because its realization would mandate resolution of fundamental issues still confronting the region.[65] In 1984 the WEU Assembly succinctly stated the reasons for this renewed interest in regional security harmonization:

(1) the military potential of the Soviet Union requires a regional balance of power resting on a unified European position;
(2) the conflict of policy outlook between the United States and Europe mandates a regional response;
(3) difficulties in realizing the goals of European integration require a return to a discussion of fundamental issues, especially defence and security;
(4) growing arms costs mean that only a regional entity will have the

economic, industrial and technological resources essential for
European firms to remain globally competitive;
(5) SDI and related topics require that Europe rethink its entire
manner and means of security policy decision-making.[66]

This study has presented the various European initiatives currently
designed to allow implementation of a harmonized regional security
policy. It remains, though, to suggest the essential bargain around
which these diverse efforts may coalesce to provide policy direction,
linkages and offsets in pursuit of a common position. The decisions
reached at the June 1985 Milan Summit of Community leaders,
although somewhat inchoate in prescription, begin to solidify the form
of a bargain whose existence until then was based mainly on tenuous
and fleeting programme strands.[67] In spite of vocal opposition from
Britain, Greece and Denmark, West Germany and France were able to
finalize plans for a new conference to pursue treaty changes consistent
with a more unified Europe. Drawing on the groundwork laid by the
Dooge Committee, this draft proposal will seek closer cooperation primarily in the areas of foreign and security policy.[68] While rejecting the
concept of a 'two-speed' Europe, proposed changes designed to
reinstate majority voting, except where vital national interests are at
stake, suggests the very real possibility that progress will be placed
above consensus in at least the foreign and security sectors. It is this primacy of the need to institute structural changes plus the implicit
acknowledgement of different rates of progress that sets this Milan
communiqué apart from similar sentiments issued at the termination
of the Paris Summit in 1972.

Although Britain agreed with the objective of harmonizing European foreign and defence policies, thus further isolating Greece and
Denmark from the mainstream of Community opinion, there is little
question but that British opposition to any greater sense of European
union remains strong. Essentially this opposition is tied to the domestic
situation in the United Kingdom where public support for the Community remains lukewarm or, among a sizeable proportion of the
population, decidedly negative. To induce British support for security
harmonization requires tangible benefits directed towards problems
facing the government and limiting its latitude to move toward a
regional accommodation. Privatization of British firms including those
active in security-related production in the hopes of rekindling their
ability to play a leading role in technologically sophisticated and competitive products has been a major economic policy thrust of the
Thatcher government. This transition in the domestic factors of production has also been mandated by the loss of labour-intensive jobs to

low-cost havens, necessitating a compensating shift in the British industrial base. Although a future Labour government might seek to terminate or reverse the move to privatization there is little short of self-defeating import barriers and massive subsidies that can offset the trend. While the union–Labour connection might require some additional measures to ease this internal transition, the inexorability of the restructuring of the international economic system will require accommodation sooner rather than later. That need then provides the point to which leverage in the form of Community resources and inducements can be successfully applied and exploited to bring about British acceptance of security-policy harmonization.

Although the Milan Summit decision on a new treaty garnered the most media attention, two other outcomes of that meeting are of longer-range importance. First was the agreement to form a committee to consider how best to formulate a European response to the French Eureka initiative. While Eureka might appear to some as yet another quixotic venture by the Community, it is viewed by others as a very real threat to the security and technology dominance of the United States. A member of the United States Air Force Secretary's office charged with, among other duties, a leading role in SDI research and development, recently noted that the emergence of Eureka as a European policy was the single most troublesome international issue facing his office.[69]

The second outcome of the Summit was the decision to complete a true internal market by 1992 at the latest. Together these two pronouncements suggest the outline of the bargain that is emerging to support Community leadership in security matters. That is the development of a regional technological base where contracts, resources and financial instruments will be available free from member strictures on their use. This base will be orientated towards the high-technology growth sectors with their dual use implications for commercial competition and security-related matters. In time this formulation will support and match the emergence of harmonized member political statements in foreign and security policy. Implementation of a Community security policy will remain subject to compromise and negotiation. Clearly, though, any policy initiative must encompass developed and proposed initiatives currently within the Community's ambit. How best, then, to refine and channel those efforts?

The pursuit of Community security harmonization should be based on what will be termed a European Technological Policy (ETP). The ETP would split the present Community industrial policy in two directions (see Figure 2) which, although complementary, are designed to

Figure 2 A Proposed European technological policy (ETP) structure

fulfil different objectives. The revised industrial policy would be directed at assisting industries in trouble, whose futures, while important from a national perspective, carry little weight within a technologically orientated region. While Community involvement would remain, it is the individual members who would carry the primary responsibility for this policy. In this fashion states such as Greece, Portugal, Spain, Italy and the United Kingdom, who deem support of sectors such as textiles and steel to be in the national interest, would be free to use national and regional resources in the manner best suited to achieve these domestically dictated goals. Regional assistance for these nationally focused programmes would be acknowledged as transitional in longevity, thus requiring participant sensitivity to the Community's primary industrial policy thrust within the ETP. Negotiated offsets between both programmes would be facilitated by this recognition.

The ETP is focused solely on firms active in the high-technology sectors whose products have dual applicability for commercial and security use. A two-tier system of management would be instituted to define, monitor and implement policy. The first policy-making tier would consist of members and Community officials in a formula to be determined. All members would be represented but a system of weighted voting calibrated to each state's contribution would be instituted. In this fashion the incentive for the larger states to increase their efforts at the expense of maintaining separate national ventures would be apparent, while a coalition of smaller members could enhance their position and their programme interest by the use of a potential veto.

The second tier consisting of Community members, with some form of advisory linkage back to members, would be charged with representing the region in external negotiations either with individual states or within other international organizations. Its role would be to implement, through negotiation and based on first-tier policy, agreements consistent with Community objectives. Experience drawn from the Commission's role in GATT and other forums would be directly relevant to the final shape of this body's competence.

The ETP's programme competence would include all current Community high-technology-orientated initiatives and programmes as well as member consortia whose purpose it is to create a European product. This latter characteristic then allows independent member pursuit of a project, such as the French Mirage, if deemed essential to national interests. Projects included in this structure would range from the Esprit through the ESA to include also any consortium developing a new European fighter (EFA). The ETP's competence would thus merge commercial and military programmes through its control over high-technology-related resources. The inclusion of the Community's MNE policy within this structure would allow members to continue their peculiar method of corporate direction yet within the policy dictates established by the ETP.

One remaining problem is the reluctance of several members to allow the Community to become involved in defence matters. Essentially three states, Denmark, Ireland and Greece, fit this profile, though for different reasons. The domestic political situation in Denmark and Greece requires both governments to minimize the perception of loss of sovereignty that would be associated with any increased Community security role. For Ireland the situation is much less fluid, grounded as it is on a neutralist foreign policy. Greek and Irish acquiescence to enlarging the Community's security responsibility could be induced by the offsets provided through the redirected industrial policy as well as by a share of the economic and commercial benefits flowing from the ETP. The matter of Danish agreement would similarly be solvable through indirect participation in the commercial aspects of the ETP and perhaps later as a purchaser of its military products. The use of EPC or WEU to mediate between the second tier of the ETP and defence transactions within NATO or export sales would shield the Community's role and allow these members, if they wish, to opt out of a direct participatory role in security matters. The proposed structure of the ETP is illustrated in Figure 2.

The suggestion of an ETP is not a panacea for the problems facing the Community. It does, however, build on current member consensus on the two issues most troublesome to Europe, commercial stature and security guarantees in a changing international system. For that reason its acceptance might be a result of more than simple academic conjecture and hope.

NOTES

1. For an overall assessment of the topic, see European Parliament Working Document, *Report on Shared European Interests, Risks and Requirements in the Security Field*, 2 April 1984, Doc. 1-80/84/B, PE 88.462/B.
2. *The International Competitive Position of European Firms*, COM(53)547, 14 September 1983, p. 1.
3. Ibid., Annex.
4. European Parliament Working Document, *Report on the Harmonization of Export Aid Systems*, 8 June 1977, Doc. 129-77, PE 47.346, p. 8.
5. 'Aiding Exporters: The EX-IM Bank's Role', in *Trade: U.S. Policy since 1945* (Washington, DC: Congressional Quarterly, Inc., 1984), pp. 187–97.
6. EC Commission, *Statute for European Companies*, April 1975 (Brussels: EC Bulletin Supplement 4/1975).
7. European Parliament Working Document, *Report on the Proposal for a Regulation setting up a European Export Bank*, 4 May 1977, Doc. 66/77, PE 42.970.
8. 'Protocol on the Statutes of the European Investment Bank', *Documents for European Community Law and Institutions*, pp. 92–9, Article 18.
9. Offical Journal of the European Communities, no. C299/2, 18 November 1980.
10. EC Commission, *The Community's Industrial Policy*, 18 March 1970 (Brussels: EC Bulletin Supplement 4/1970), p. 19.
11. Ibid., p. 56.
12. European Parliament Working Document, *Report for a Regulation on the European Cooperation Grouping (ECG)*, 21 January 1977, Doc. 519/76, PE 43.059, pp. 1–32.
13. EC Commission, *A Four-Year Programme for the Development of Informatics in the Community*, COM(76)524 final, 29 October 1976, vol. I, pp. 40–6 (hereafter *Informatics Study*).
14. Harment Lehment, 'The European Monetary System' in Leon Hurwitz, ed., *The Harmonization of European Public Policy* (Westport, CT: Greenwood Press, 1983), pp. 183–96.
15. EC Commission, *Towards Community Financing of Innovations in Small and Medium-Sized Enterprises*, COM(83)241, 7 June 1983.
16. Ibid., Article 2.
17. Ibid., part IV, 1(b).
18. Ibid., part IV, 1(c).
19. EC Commission, *Proposal Adopting the first European Strategic Programme for Research and Development in Information Technologies (ESPRIT)*, COM(83)258, 2 June 1983, pp. 1–5 (hereafter *Esprit Programme*).
20. Ibid., p. 8.
21. 'Investing in Europe's Future', *European Investment Bank*, no. 38 (April 1984), p. 1.
22. *The European Community's Industrial Strategy*, periodical 5/1982 (Brussels: European Documents, 1982), p. 52.

23. Stephen Woolcock, 'Information Technology: The Challenge to Europe', *Journal of Common Market Studies*, 22, 4 (June 1984), pp. 315–31.
24. 'Summary of Vice President Davignon's Speech Delivered at the Financial Times Conference on World Electronics', press release, 22 June 1984, IP(84)222, pp. 1–2.
25. *Esprit Programme*, COM(83)258, p. 3.
26. *On Improving the International Competitive Position of European Firms*, COM(83)547.
27. *The European Community and New Technologies*, April 1984, p. 5.
28. Ibid., p. 6.
29. EC Commission, *Community Actions in the Field of Microelectronic Technology*, second report by the Commission, COM(84)567, 23 October 1984.
30. Ibid., p. 19.
31. Ibid., p. 21.
32. 'European Software Agreement', *New York Times*, 19 February 1985, p. 29.
33. *Informatics Study*, Annex.
34. 'European Fighter Project Competes with U.S. Firms', *Europe*, March/April 1985, pp. 16–17.
35. *Multinational Coproduction of Military Aerospace Systems*, R-2861-AF (Santa Monica, CA: Rand, 1981).
36. 'European Fighter Project Competes with U.S. Firms', pp. 16–17.
37. Ibid.
38. 'Greece Complains of Delay in U.S. Approval of F-16 Sale', *Air Force Times*, 2 September 1985, p. 36.
39. 'On a Wing and a Computer', *The Economist*, 10 August 1985, p. 34.
40. Assembly of Western European Union, *United States–European Cooperation in Advanced Technology*, 30th ordinary session, 2nd part, 8 November 1984, Doc. 992.
41. Werner Kaltefleiter, *The Strategic Defense Initiative: Some Implications for Europe* (London: Institute for European Defence and Strategic Studies, occasional paper 10, February 1985).
42. 'Mitterrand, Kohl Meet on "Star Wars"', *The Washington Post*, 1 March 1985, p. 12.
43. ' "Star Wars" Is the Big Issue in Bonn', *New York Times*, 1 May 1985, p. 8; 'Star Wars Debate Reveals Split Coalition', *The German Tribune*, 28 April 1985, p. 3.
44. 'High Tech at the Summit', *New York Times*, 22 April 1985, p. 23.
45. 'Kohl Supports U.S. over "Star Wars" ', *New York Times*, 19 April 1985, p. 4.
46. 'Manna from Heaven', *The Economist*, 27 April 1985, pp. 18–19.
47. 'The Reticent Seven', *The Economist*, 27 April 1985, pp. 60 and 65.
48. 'Western Europe Decides to Pull Together on Defense research', *Christian Science Monitor*, 28 June 1985, p. 9.
49. 'European Project Picks up Support', *New York Times*, 26 May 1985, p. 7.
50. 'U.S. Space Programs: Cooperation and Competition from Europe', *Current Policy*, 695 (Washington, DC: US Department of State, 1985).
51. Roy Gibson, 'Aerospatial Cooperation: The European Space Agency', in Hurwitz, *Harmonization of European Public Policy*, p. 55.
52. Ibid., p. 55.
53. Ibid., pp. 59–9.
54. 'Europe v. NASA in Space', *The Gazette* (Colorado Springs), 14 April 1985, p. F5.
55. Assembly of Western European Union, *Military Use of Space, Part II*, 30th ordinary session, 2nd part, 8 November 1984, Doc. 993.
56. 'Europe v. NASA in Space', p. F5.
57. 'U.S. Space Programs: Cooperation and Competition from Europe'.
58. 'Europe's Chance to Climb aboard the Space Station', *The Economist*, 15 December 1984, pp. 103–4.

108   *The coalescing of a European security policy*

59. Gibson, 'Aerospatial Cooperation: The European Space Agency', p. 80.
60. EC Commission, *Remote Sensing from Space*, EUR 8039 EN.
61. Richard Feld, 'Corporate Sovereignty', *Columbia Journal of World Business*, 5 (August 1970), pp. 66–82.
62. Philippe Lemaitre and Catherine Goybet, *Les Entreprises multinationales dans la Communauté Européenne* (Geneva: PUF, 1984); EC Commission, *Lavori della CCE che possono riguardare la società multinazionali*, 17 January 1977 (Brussels: III/164/77-I), pp. 1–44.
63. Ronald Coleman, 'Community Law and Codes of Conduct for Multinational Enterprises', position paper for EC Industrial Commissioner Davignon, 22 December 1978.
64. Selected personal interviews with NATO flight officers, not for attribution.
65. Bernard Burrows and Geoffrey Edwards, *The Defence of Western Europe* (London: Butterworth Scientific, 1982); Baard Bredrup Knudsen, *Europe versus America: Foreign Policy in the 1980s* (Paris: The Atlantic Institute for International Affairs, 1984).
66. Assembly of Western European Union, *Thirty Years of the Modified Brussels Treaty*, 30th ordinary session, 1st part, 15 May 1984, Doc. 973, p. 23.
67. 'European Community pulls off a surprise in Milan', *The German Tribune*, 7 July 1985, p. 1.
68. 'European Council of Heads of State and Government—Dublin, December 3/4', *European Report*, 1 December 1984.
69. Personal interviews, not for attribution.

6 A new European security policy: the choice of institution

The need to structure the Western response to the military and ideological challenges posed by the Soviet Union is generally acknowledged to require some form of coordinating mechanism. A structure simply integrating Allied military forces in response to an attack is neither functional nor reflective of the nature of the commitment underlying the Atlantic Alliance. The forty years of post-World War Two peace in Europe is in no small sense due to the enlargement of the tasks performed by the militarily focused NATO alliance. Standardization of weapons and the need to maintain a public supportive of the Alliance has added political and economic tasks to the ongoing military sense of mission for transatlantic cohesion within NATO.

The Alliance does not, however, exist in a vacuum separate from the issues and tensions of the times. This dynamic of balancing long-term military tasks within the changing short-term political and economic environment is the challenge. To assume that only NATO can fulfil that function is to lose sight of these underlying currents. The ability to structure a coherent Western response is further complicated by the perceptible change of member attitudes on the manner best suited to direct East–West relations. While few members still subscribe to conflict management through an 'end of ideology' thesis, clear divisions remain, more prevalent across the Atlantic than within Europe, concerning acceptable limits on Western concessions in the hope of realigning the Soviet Union towards a more pacific view of international security matters. John Van Oudenaren's typology of alternative approaches to East–West relations clearly articulates and nicely differentiates these distinct policy options.[1] He suggests that American–Soviet relations may be characterized by one of three approaches, each of which gives rise to differing means and methods of directing those interactions. He calls the three options: termination by accommodation; termination by victory; and long-term conflict management.[2] While it is simplistic to assume that the United States and each of the European NATO members neatly fits one category or other, it is also fatuous to dismiss clearly held and often contradictory views on the management of East–West relations.

In sum, structuring Alliance relations is not simply an institutional exercise. Competing policy approaches, whether military, political or economic, require organizational flexibility yet within the dictates of ultimate purpose. Simple military preparedness does not suffice. To be effective both as to process and purpose, any institutional framework must acknowledge and hopefully solve the following sets of Alliance issues and concerns:

(1) common military strategy;
(2) geographic limits and membership;
(3) defence procurement (the 'two-way street');
(4) monetary resources and contributions.

It has often been suggested that while NATO might not be a perfect solution, it is better than any other alternative. In an Alliance relationship grounded on American power and global hegemony that assessment was probably correct. But that dominance no longer exists and indeed asymmetries in the total transatlantic balance at times favour the European partners at the expense of the United States. It is appropriate, therefore, once again to raise the institutional question previously addressed by the EDC and the MLF, keeping in mind the structural changes within the Alliance mandating not only this reappraisal but also a reassessment of the European role within that equation. Since there is little desire to create a new organization for this purpose each of these four issues will be assessed within the three leading candidates for directing change: NATO; Western European Union (WEU); and the European Community (EC).

NATO: A POST-WAR ANOMALY?

For almost four decades NATO has served as the visible commitment of the United States to the defence of Western interests in Europe. Among the acronyms spawned by Kennan's containment policy, NATO alone has managed intra-Alliance as well as inter-bloc relations with a fair measure of success. A large degree of credit for this success must be attributed to its essentially political rationale and therefore attentiveness and sensitivity to non-military issues. Whether providing the opportunity for a militarily revitalized West Germany or eliciting public support in pursuit of INF deployments, much of NATO's success has been as a direct outcome of its extra-military functions. But this politicization of tasks has also increased organizational visibility and presence in a manner not always conducive to the effective implementation of its primary military role. It is without question that a political role is essential to the development of a security policy. It is not equally clear that NATO is able to perform these four roles in a fashion conducive to the creation of a coherent security policy for Europe.

A common military strategy

Political divisions in the Alliance on the nature of the Soviet threat have been translated into disagreement over appropriate NATO strategy. Any change in NATO doctrine, as demonstrated by protracted debate over the 1967 substitution of flexible response for massive retaliation, is difficult to adopt, let alone implement, even when reflective of member consensus on its utility. When consensus does not exist, when change is pursuant to the wishes of the dominant member or when change signals an abrupt departure in policy, then the potential for divisiveness dramatically increases. That sense of division is what permeates NATO today.

SDI, FOFA and ETs are policy changes pursued by the United States consistent with its general strategic shift away from deterrence towards a war-fighting capability in the European area. It is precisely these weapons and the aggressive strategy for their use that disturbs Europeans and which has prompted a major division over the proper posture to assume to counter the threat, as now perceived, issuing from the Soviet Union.

Although defensive in nature, NATO has never dismissed the militarily opportune need to interdict Warsaw Pact forces before they enter West Germany. 'Deep interdiction', striking the second echelon of attack, although recently restated in the Air-Land battle scenario, is not a new idea.[3] There is, though, a subtle political distinction between interdiction in support of a defensive posture and what has been termed by Samuel Huntington as the need to increase NATO's operational credibility through the adoption of a 'conventional retaliation' strategy.[4] Conventional retaliation is quite simply the effort to convince the Eastern Europeans not to invade NATO territory for fear of reciprocal conventional thrusts into their own areas. A militarily sound strategy whether labelled offensive or defensive is none the less viewed by many European NATO members as politically unworkable, connoting a shift from a deterrent or passive role to one of active offence. Rather than using the path of détente, however defined, to restrain and redirect East European priorities, conventional retaliation suggests a return to Van Oudenaren's termination by victory whose underlying rationale is inconsistent with current and apparently long-term European attitudes.

Geographic limits and membership constraints

Further complicating intra-NATO policy coherence are the geographic limits placed on its mandate. Article 6 of the NATO treaty limits the geographic scope for possible intervention essentially to an attack on the territory of armed forces of the signatories. Notwithstanding the official explanation of this article, that events outside of the area may still be a subject of consultation or action for the Alliance, out-of-area issue management remains one of the major banes for NATO planners.[5] Vestiges of Vietnam and the American penchant to view its security commitments as global have essentially limited NATO actions to a regional scope. Clearly outside that boundary lie the Middle East oil supplies vital to the economic well-being of Western Europe. The extent of the NATO commitment to protect these sources is an agreement by West Germany to recall reservists to the Central Front in the event of an American draw-down on their forces for temporary use in the oil fields. This is not to suggest the lack of interest or military assets by NATO members such as France or Italy in the continuation of those supplies, but rather an unwillingness to increase NATO's area of responsibility for fear of setting a precedent that might then be expanded under American pressure to areas such as Africa or Central America.[6]

This antipathy towards expanding NATO's area of responsibility is usually attributed to the parochial views and limited assets of European NATO members. A more attractive explanation would suggest that this reluctance is due instead to European fears that, once enlargement were undertaken, American preponderance of assets would ensure leadership and thus policy direction according to its unilaterally determined objectives. It is fear of loss of political control over the action rather than timidity over such excursions that restrains European members. French actions in Chad, the British excursion to the Falklands and the Italian expansion of its Mediterranean maritime role, demonstrate the assets and the will for intervention when in the interests of the states involved.

NATO cohesion is also complicated by the nature of its membership. Greek–Turkish antagonism repeatedly illuminated over Cyprus is but one of these concerns. The role of Spain is perhaps more illustrative of the problem. The American desire for Spanish NATO membership is essentially a strategic one, given the latter's control of the approaches to the Western Mediterranean and its potential as a staging area to resupply the German Central Front.[7] Spain's rationale for membership is instead economic, viewing its support of NATO as the entry fee to the markets, resources and assistance held out by other European members. Spanish, Portuguese and Greek military contributions to NATO, other than the perceptual signal of a common Western stance, are minimal, reflecting limited resources but more importantly a less than striking sense of the Soviet threat. Indeed the Southern tier of NATO, with the exception of Italy and Turkey, are negligible military actors in the Alliance and pursue foreign policies that deviate often in significant measure from that of the United States.[8] Spanish and Greek disputes over American basing rights and their disagreement with President Reagan's Central American policy are but visible reminders of these differences. It is unlikely that these states will become more excited about increasing or even maintaining their defence commitments as long as that organization's objectives are so closely directed by American foreign policy goals.

Defence procurement and the NATO 'two-way' street

Perhaps the most pressing economic concern in peacetime NATO are the asymmetries present in the 'two-way street' designed to fulfil intra-Alliance defence procurement requirements in a more equitable fashion[9]. Alliance military procurement decisions remain the province of national governments but may be denominated as 'NATO projects' if the following conditions are met:

(1) the participation of two or more NATO members;
(2) an agreement to report annually on the progress of the project until the equipment has been produced or the project ended; and
(3) the incorporation of a provision for the admittance of other interested NATO states in the future.[10]

Although numerous collaborative efforts are termed NATO projects most analysts, including Allied military officers, would agree with the assessment that, 'in general the NATO project designation is of little significance'.[11] Clearly national control of a project is the overriding concern since members view employment, national mission and protection of the domestic industrial base as priorities. The technological prowess, industrial capacity and global mission of the United States, when combined with this desire for national control, are the major reasons for the asymmetry in current intra-NATO sales and transfers.

European NATO members have struggled to find a means to redress this inequality. Dismissing the option of complete dependence on American products, either as outright purchases or under licence, as damaging to their own objectives has done much to exacerbate the achievement of the militarily desirable objectives of standardization and interoperability. National projects such as the British Harrier remain possible but the minimal requirements of national forces require foreign sales in order to maintain the profitability of the venture. European collaborative ventures including the Lynx–Puma–Gazelle helicopters, the Hot–Milan–Roland missiles and the Tornado have been pursued as a means of ensuring extranational sales in order to maintain domestic production lines and meet national military requirements. But even this intra-European cooperation has yet to realign the inequities present in American–European sales balances. Even when one eliminates high-cost strategic systems such as the Trident submarine, Europe still has been unable to convince the United States of the need to 'buy European'. The introduction of co-ordinating mechanisms such as the Eurogroup and the IEPG, although successful in rationalizing intra-NATO requirements and eliminating duplication of efforts, has had little impact on increasing American willingness to forgo their products in favour of European ones.[12]

The problem of sales equity rests precisely on the fact that these alternatives are not truly European ventures but *ad hoc* efforts designed to achieve national objectives at less cost. There does not exist a European entity with the power to define projects, allocate responsibility and ensure implementation free from governmental intervention. This absence then redounds to render ineffective European NATO member efforts to convince the United States to purchase its products.

Member resources and contributions

The final and perhaps most sensitive intra-Alliance topic is the question of monetary and resource contributions to NATO. Usually addressed under the rubric of 'burden-sharing' the issue is more simply seen as one of fairness. The Nunn Amendment, seeking a reduction of American NATO troops if European contributions were not dramatically increased, is the United States' counterpart to Europe's plea of insufficient resources given the twin constraints of social obligations and an uneven economy. The 1979 NATO decision to seek a 3 per cent real increase in defence spending by members was an effort to defuse this issue by setting a figure low enough to be attainable in Europe yet high enough to quell American criticism.[13] The ability of NATO, though not of all members, to achieve that figure (see Table 13) did minimize at least in the short term American calls for more drastic action.

Table 13. NATO country defence spending: percentage change from previous year in constant prices (excluding in Ratio)

	1978 or 1978–79	1979 or 1979–80	1980 or 1980–81	1981 or 1981–82
Belgium	6.7	2.2	2.0	0.2
Canada[1]	−.2	−.9	5.1	3.0
Denmark	4.4	.2	.7	.1
France	5.0	2.5	3.9	3.5
Germany	3.1	1.8	1.9	1.9/3.4
Greece	4.9	−2.9	−8.8	5.6
Italy	1.4	2.6	4.9	−1.2
Luxembourg	7.9	3.5	16.3	7.1
Netherlands	−4.8	3.9	−1.5	2.3/3.4
Norway	7.7	1.9	1.8	2.5
Portugal	2.4	2.9	10.1	2.8
Turkey[1]	0	2.6	2.0	3.1
United Kingdom[1]	−.6	3.0	2.7	2.1
	1977–78	1978–79	1979–80	1980–81
United States[1]	1.5	3.4	4.9	5.4
Non-United States[2]	2.1	2.2	2.6	2.2/2.6
NATO total[2]	1.8	2.9	3.8	4.0/4.1

[1] All of the figures depicted in this table are based on the NATO definition of defence spending and are the best estimates that can be made on the basis of information now available. Nation fiscal years agree to calendar years except as follows: Canada and United Kingdom—April–March. Turkey—March–February. United States—October–September.
[2] Non-United States NATO and NATO totals reflect weighted average growth rates.
Source: U.S. Government.

The issue of burden-sharing is difficult to assess because so many non-monetary factors must be included in the equation. A 1984 West German publication includes under the heading 'other contributions' factors such as lost rental revenue on land provided to NATO and reimbursement for damage to civilian property caused by Allied manœuvres.[14] Each European member makes similar claims. Notwithstanding the difficulty of ascribing an exact figure to contributions there are several accepted methods for assessing overall expenditures.

The commonly used measure of burden-sharing is the percentage of the gross domestic product (GDP) allocated to defense. This indicator ... has the major shortcoming of failing to consider the heavy socialization of the European economies, the uneven effects of inflation and currency fluctuations. It also fails to take into account the ability of a country to pay—a prime concern when the objective is the equitable distribution of the burden [see Table 14].[15]

Table 14. Burden sharing

	% of GDP on Defense	Rank[1]	Per Capita GDP	Rank[2]
US	6.9	2	13,098	1
Belgium	3.4	5–7	7,812	6
Denmark	2.5	10	10,949	3
France	4.2	4	8,812	5
W. Germany	3.4	5–7	10,970	2
Italy	2.8	9	5,974	8
Holland	3.3	8	9,766	4
UK	5.6	3	7,200	7
Greece	7.1	1	3,724	10
Spain	2.1	11	4,154	9
Portugal	3.4	5–7	1,506	11

[1] SIPRI Yearbook 1984, p. 127
[2] International Financial Statistics, Yearbook, 1983, IMF

To redress this inequity an alternative computing technique is utilized which is grounded on two assumptions: first, that defence spending should be directly proportional to some measure of relative affluence and, second, that the American spending performance may be taken as the 'standard' against which to measure all other contributions (see Table 15).

The second column in Table 15, calculated upon the equity perspective that those more able should contribute more, yields only one surprise, that of West Germany. While the low figures from Denmark and the Netherlands may be explained by recourse to the

Table 15. Comparison of defence burdens

	% of GDP	Proportion to square of per capita GDP
US	1.00	1.00
Belgium	0.49	0.82
Denmark	0.36	0.43
France	0.61	0.91
W. Germany	0.49	0.59
Italy	0.41	0.89
Holland	0.48	0.64
UK	0.81	1.48
Greece	1.03	3.60
Spain	0.30	0.96
Portugal	0.49	4.30

dictates of a sensitive political environment, the 0.59 figure for West Germany cannot be dismissed for similar reasons. It is more likely that the West German contribution could be raised but in so doing would so dwarf the total contributions of other European NATO members as to be politically prohibitive. In that case the West German concern to make known its other non-financial contributions takes on added importance.

The figures also suggest that the American feeling of having unfairly to shoulder the NATO burden might have to be rethought. The American desire for increased European contributions is stronger when based on the technique utilized in the first column. But the political realities of budgetary contributions strongly suggest that as long as one computing technique yields results sympathetic to the European position American calls for individual or overall increases will fall on deaf ears. Instead emphasis must be directed to the output side of the equation, in essence how to spend available resources in a more efficient manner.

Thomas A. Callaghan, Jr, one of the most vocal and respected of Alliance analysts, addressed this topic most recently in June 1984.[16] Callaghan notes that 'even when governments are spending more money to rearm, disarmament occurs' because the increased unit cost of weapons means that fewer weapons may be produced.[17] This 'structural disarmament' will continue until 'NATO governments establish an intercontinental market structure for the production and exchange of armaments'. Callaghan lays out seven steps that must ensue to implement this objective, all of which are grounded on the need for European NATO members to join together to fashion a second pillar in the procurement two-way street. He concludes that '[a] European Defence Industrial Community . . . will have to be established . . . which will insure the participation of all 13 armed European members of the Alliance'.[18]

Strong support for Callaghan's prescriptions is found in both the Eurogroup and the IEPG[19]. Although the economic arguments for European cooperation are impeccable they are also seen by interested parties as floundering on political issues. The difficulties of translating economic efficiency into political policy even at national level is nicely illustrated by the recent decision on the American B-1 bomber. In order to ensure sufficient political weight to offset any future production cutbacks, parts of the B-1 are to be made in virtually all of the fifty states. Such politicization of programmes is magnified when the scope of the issue moves beyond the national arena. Thus it is a matter of national will, in the best sense of the term 'politics', that ultimately will determine the feasibility of Callaghan's suggestions. The opportunity for NATO to structure that discussion, which will require agenda management in areas far out of its accepted mandate, is therefore highly suspect.

THE COMMON MARKET AS THE NEW FOCAL POINT FOR EUROPEAN SECURITY POLICY

It is simplistic to assert and it will not be argued that NATO is no longer capable of performing its mission and thus must be dismantled. The vitality of that organization is due in no small measure to its role as a sounding-board for member concerns, channelling disagreement and pursuing compromise within established and accepted institutional parameters. The problem is not with NATO as an institution, but rather with NATO as the means of pursuing negotiations within an environment characterized as one of complex interdependence.

NATO was designed to manage an asymmetric relationship both within the Alliance and between it and the competing Eastern bloc. The past crises it has weathered reflect the external changes underway as a more equal balance is thrust on both these aspects of NATO relations. The current issue is how to reorganize that institution internally so that Alliance management may be viewed as a cooperative venture rather than as an extension of American foreign policy initiatives. A more equitable distribution of power, although compatible with peacetime activities, does leave open the question of battle management should hostilities break out. Any realignment must also incorporate the effects of sensitivity and vulnerability dependence on any new or redefined Alliance arrangement. Thus the following sections on European alternatives to the present NATO system are designed to query the feasibility of three separate options:

(1) the ability to realign the internal sharing of power within NATO;
(2) the possibility and efficacy of establishing a true European pillar within NATO;
(3) the option for a separate European defence organization somewhat allied to NATO.

WEU and the European Community (EC) are inextricably linked with the post-World War Two search for some form of European political, economic and perhaps military union. In 1952 the ECSC, experimental and transitional in conception, was the initial step toward rejoining the fragmented sovereignties of a resurgent Europe. While successful in its immediate economic goals, the ECSC's great contribution was the resolution of decades of Franco-German animosity, clearing the way for a strengthened Europe firmly grounded on the core of this rapprochement. The military path for defence cooperation was paved by the 1948 Brussels Treaty establishing the Western Union Defence Organization (WUDO), which later became the WEU. Upon the signing of the NATO treaty on 20 December 1950, WUDO agreed to transfer its military responsibilities to NATO to avoid duplication of efforts and to acknowledge the primacy of the latter organization which was grounded on American participation and support.[20]

At the same time the closer relations between WUDO and NATO members would be continued through the automatic obligation to aid in case of attack contained in the Brussels Treaty. Even at this early date the sense that NATO was not enough permeated European views. This sense of the necessity of greater European defence cooperation, paralleled in the economic sphere by the ECSC, led to the French proposal for a European Army. The Pleven Plan was viewed as a necessary step towards European integration by terminating the artificial separation between defence and political and economic planning. The Plan further allowed the reintroduction of West Germany into Europe and secured its passivity by membership in both the ECSC and the newly proposed European Defence Community (EDC). The EDC treaty was signed on 27 May 1952 by the original ECSC members and was accompanied by separate protocols linking EDC members to both the UK and NATO.[21]

The failure of the French Assembly on 30 August 1954 to ratify the EDC treaty now required that the issues of German rearmament and European defence be separated from political and economic matters. The 1954 London Conference transferred the issues of German remilitarization and European defence to the NATO agenda and set the pattern for European acquiescence to the United States in security matters. This separation became complete when the 1955 Messina Conference established the framework for the Common Market, ensuring that European preoccupation would be inward and focused on the development of economic links within the security environment now left to American guidance.

Although security policy was now distinct from Community political and economic development, there remained the recognition that the European NATO role and the objectives of programme coherence within the Community required a policy vehicle that could bridge that gap.[22] That objective was gradually, though incompletely, recognized by efforts to standardize NATO arms requirements and production to give European members a greater share of available contracts. Several agencies were established to direct that objective, among which the more successful have been the Eurogroup, the IEPG and the Standing

Armaments Committee (SAC). Although successful in standardizing system requirements, they have been totally unable to integrate the production capabilities of European members in order to increase their ability to attract NATO contracts. Some although not all of the problem has been the success of American MNEs in attracting European partners for proposed contracts, thus negating the opportunity for joint European development and production of alternative systems at competitive prices. A greater difficulty is that the exclusion of private firms from these agencies ensures that negotiations are intergovernmental, with politically sensitive concerns such as employment overriding the short-term ability to seek agreement to enhance the European role within the NATO sales environment.

The Community has been somewhat more successful in its support of European consortia desirous of competing in global markets. The success of the Airbus consortium is grounded on cooperation between private, national and regional actors in pursuit of sales opportunities particularly at the expense of American firms such as Boeing. But the separation between military and civilian matters does not allow Community involvement in projects such as the Tornado which remain *ad hoc* arrangements at national and private levels. The result is that NATO-related agencies such as the SAC have the legitimacy to address European cooperation but lack any ability to do so, while the Community has the ability but lacks the legitimacy. The vehicle that would allow the Community to expand its agenda to address defence projects in order to minimize resource waste and maximize the applicability of results was presented in the discussion in Chapter 5 of a European technological policy. The introduction of a European technological policy geared to cooperation in pursuit of 'dual use' items would then serve as the bridge allowing security issues to be brought within the Community's ambit. In addition a ETP would allow the four challenges now facing NATO to be resolved in a more equitable, permanent and European-directed fashion.

A European military strategy

Since the Community is not able to assume the role of security planning, even when its own survival is at stake, some combination of NATO, regional and national planning must coexist to assure implementation of policy requirements.[23] But security is not simply a military concern, reflecting as it does the political concept of public support and the economic sense of planning efficiency. It is here that a renewed European spirit has its place. As previously detailed, the ability of Europe to discuss its security concerns was minimized by events leading to the emphasis instead on political and economic initiatives. Yet current movement on such matters focusing on a new federally orientated treaty continue to flounder on British, Greek and Danish reluctance to move toward the political vision of unity without first finalizing and realizing benefits from current economic programmes. Ironically, then, the sense of movement in Europe has now swung to defence and security matters. At the termination of the 1985 Milan European Council meeting the United Kingdom strongly opposed any move towards federalism, yet 'called on all members to agree on new procedures for harmonizing their foreign and defence policies'.[24] That suggestion mirrors sentiments held not only by France and West Germany but also by WEU as a whole.[25] It is insufficient to suggest that this British turnaround in policy priorities is an effort to move away from the objective of federalism by focusing on more immediate but equally unattainable topics. Rather it is an acknowledgement that union, however defined, may not exist separately from security and defence matters. To pursue an institutional and policy role in security matters is therefore to pursue the objective of union but from less elusive grounds. Political decisions to include a security dimension will be required to structure these cooperative economic outcomes. What then might the British recommendation portend in the area of a harmonized security policy? It would be an extravagant leap of faith to infer a desire for shared nuclear ownership or even European planning on strategic forces. Instead two other possibilities—a common operational strategy and cooperative procurement planning— are more likely avenues to pursue.

A recent British White Paper on Defence acknowledges that over the next decade the upgrading of their strategic force through the purchase of the Trident system will require a diminution of the funds available to other military sectors.[26] Since the British Army of the Rhine (BAOR) and a 'blue water' navy account, along with the strategic force, for the bulk of expenditures it is expected that cuts will be felt in those areas. The Navy has already been scaled back to the point where it will function mainly in an anti-submarine warfare (ASW) capacity along approach points to the British Isles and Northern Europe. United Kingdom force commitments of 55,000 men and the 2nd Tactical Air Force to West Germany have also been diminished and, some analysts suggest, will be reduced further to a level of about 15,000 men by 1990.[27] Thus the pre-eminence accorded to strategic forces suggests an inability to acquiesce to current American operational plans for a war-fighting capability in NATO and an increased willingness to associate more closely with the prevailing European perspective for increasing deterrence. The special relationship between Britain and the United

States, long a barrier to increased European military and security planning, can therefore be expected gradually to diminish. The question of whether closer European cooperation or an isolationist British posture will result from these events will depend in great measure on the outcome of the domestic battle between the Labour and Conservative parties in future elections. If the former is the case then the British arsenal may at some future time become associated with that of the French in pursuit of a European strategic and intermediate capability supporting conventional forces of members such as West Germany. Notwithstanding this assessment, steps toward transferring this capability to a European entity remain a matter of conjecture at this time.

A second outcome suggested by limited British defence resources underscores the need to increase its share of NATO procurement contracts in support of industrial capability. Although innovative in design and technical refinement, British products suffer from an inability to sell at a competitive price, essentially because of high labour costs. After developing the Harrier 'jump jet' for use by British forces, continuation of production lines was made possible only by a major purchase by the United States Marine Corps. A by-product of the sale was that British firms were to become subcontractors on their own design to the American firm of McDonnell Douglas. A desire to exploit its innovations and thus derive the maximum of revenue has led to a renewed British interest in joint projects with other European firms and governments. British partnership in the Tornado and its proposed successor, the European Fighter Aircraft (EFA), has enabled it to participate as a major partner with other Europeans rather than as a subcontractor to an American firm. The greater compatibility between British and other European states in terms of employment practices, costing and marketing suggests a greater opportunity for long-term security cooperation arrangements in the future.

Geographic limits and membership constraints

WEU and the Community are purely European entities thus immediately dispelling intra-NATO tensions engendered by American membership. Further Community membership firmly grounded on a politico-economic basis far less narrow than the military foundation of NATO is able to manage agendas and interactions as a primary rather than a derivative function. Although militarily orientated, WEU's current rationale has also shifted to the politico-economic sphere as planning functions have superseded defence guarantees over the years.

Current movement toward a European security policy is a function and a response to the nature of membership within both WEU and the

Community.[28] At the November 1981 London Conference it was acknowledged that overlap between foreign and security issues necessitated the latter's inclusion within the EPC process. The 1981 Genscher–Colombo proposal and the 1984 Dooge Committee sought to pursue the non-military aspects of security planning within EPC but were blocked by the reluctance of several members, including the United Kingdom, to enlarge the EC's policy mandate. The Community's requirement of consensus backed by the threat of a formal veto has necessitated that an alternative forum be found. It is for this reason that the WEU has emerged as the entity within which efforts to devise a sense of European solidarity on security matters have been pursued.

The resurgence of WEU has been facilitated by its membership, which does not include, with the exception of the United Kingdom, any Community member reluctant to discuss security concerns. This symbiosis between EPC and WEU was explicit in the final communiqué issued at the latter's 1984 Rome Conference.[29] It was stated that WEU's twin objectives were to increase European security cooperation as a balance against American domination of NATO as well as to provide a coordinating mechanism to members who sought but were unable to achieve a similar solution within either EPC or the EC. WEU's objective of a coordinated European security structure but without the explicit policy entanglements engendered by Community deliberations allows the opportunity to thrash out options in a manner not available within the EC.

British reluctance to pursue such discussions, although still visible within WEU, is minimized by the inchoate nature of that institution which emphasizes voluntary adherence to specific agreement rather than steady progress toward some defined endpoint of unity. A 'two-speed' approach to WEU initiatives does not carry the same negative connotations as it does within the Community yet might set the example for later participation for now reluctant members such as the United Kingdom.

Aside from its role in managing Community relations, a WEU–EPC combination is also integral to intra-NATO issue management. France's direct participation and indeed leadership in WEU–EPC's nascent security role ends the artificiality of soliciting its inputs through the IEPG. The uniquely European posture of this institutional combination then lends itself towards resolution of the geographic membership constraints faced within NATO. The exclusion of NATO southern and northern flank members from the WEU, although inimical to Alliance planning, enhances the coherence of remaining member initiatives. The peripheral military contribution of these excluded members suggests that the loss of the institution is essentially a perceptual one because their absence lessens the external validation of WEU initiatives. This loss, though, is more than compensated for by the ability of WEU members to reach agreement consistent with and reflective of the need for a European security policy in the short term.

Defence procurement and the NATO 'two-way' street

The inability of NATO to pursue joint production of armaments stems from two distinct but interrelated reasons. First, the American position which acknowledges the economic benefits of cooperation but within a structure heavily skewed toward its own domestic industries. Although based on the militarily sound principle of defence production removed from the potential battlefield, it is viewed instead by Europeans as a continued effort to ensure economic and technological domination. Second, the European penchant for *ad hoc* intergovernmental agreement on specific projects rather than a truly coordinated industrial policy with long-term planning and shared resource commitments. Although functional specialization or the assignment of production responsibility by the weapons sector to each member has repeatedly been proposed as an equitable solution, it continues to flounder on domestic pressures to retain a capability in employment-intensive, prestige industrial sectors supportive of an independent defence structure no matter how costly, wasteful or duplicative.[30] Yet the benefits of specialization, efficiency, and sufficiency on limited defence budgets are not lightly dismissed. Lacking, though, is the stimulus to effect such coordination.

The need for a policy framework with sufficient political clout to pursue the economically and industrially desirable objectives of cooperation would be credibly met through a Community technological policy. As previously discussed, the ETP's emphasis on the dual use of high-technology growth sectors suggests the opportunity to embrace at some future point the specifically military aspects of this issue. The short-term requirement is then for a bridge combining the industrial resources of Community members within a political framework that is able to deal directly with defence-related topics. That function could be performed through the expansion of the role of the WEU's Standing Armaments Committee (SAC). Over the past decades the SAC has relinquished many of its original planning functions to the IEPG or the Eurogroup, concerning itself instead with studies on the general aspects of member armaments industries.

At the 12 June 1984 WEU ministerial meeting it was proposed to expand SAC's role as a vehicle to channel Europe's response to the military-technological issues facing them as a result of American initiatives. Specifically the SAC is to 'ensure a link between industries and governments to provide a meeting ground for those taking part in co-production'.[31] Additionally, the SAC has been prompted by various NATO groups to assume a more visible and initiatory role in military procurement matters. The NATO objective is to share its workload with the SAC, with the latter concentrating on intra-European procurement matters. One of the coordinating functions that could be undertaken by the SAC is the industrial planning required to implement the October 1984 suggestion by two French generals for a European observation satellite.[32] The fact that the commercial aspects of satellite use are already being pursued within the Community's industrial policy and the compatible ESA would provide an easily accessible institutional entry point for cooperation with the SAC. In turn this coordination of military functions within the SAC could easily be expanded or assimilated into some version of Klepsch's EAPA. In so doing the current inefficiencies of intergovernmental agreement could be replaced by a central coordinating mechanism pursuing industrial-military cooperation within the political parameters decided at EPC and WEU levels. In this fashion the position of Europe within NATO would be buoyed by internal arrangements firmly grounded on regional rather than simply national objectives.

Monetary and resource contributions for security

Professor Hedley Bull has stated that '[t]here is no objective or material reason why Western Europe cannot provide the resources for its own security without depending on others; the reasons why it has failed to do so are not material but spiritual or psychological'.[33] Indeed, with a Western European population of approximately 370 million and a gross domestic product approaching $3,000 billion, Professor Bull's assessment would appear sound. While this study agrees with his conclusion, the question remains whether it is possible to translate the potential held out by these assets into tangible resources dedicated to a European defence and security system. That ability, in turn, will determine the shape of any European security effort and suggest what, if any, role must still be assumed by the United States within the NATO structure.

Philip Towle has persuasively argued that Europe alone cannot field sufficient forces without American assistance in order credibly to offset the Warsaw Pact capability.[34] Although sound, Towle's argument is based on a static comparison of European NATO forces to those of the Eastern bloc and does not go far enough to engage the dynamic qualities of the Alliance. Instead the question must shift from a focus on internal European capability to the external demands imposed on Europe which increasingly narrow the security options open to the region. Earl Ravenal, writing in *Foreign Affairs*, has also assessed this question and concludes that its resolution will be determined by what he terms the 'devolution' of the American commitment to Europe.[35] Predicated on the need to reduce military costs and curtail global defence commitments, Ravenal suggests an American policy of non-intervention grounded on two salient characteristics: credibility and feasibility. The essence of the new American strategy for Europe are ground assets backed by a dyad of nuclear capable submarines and cruise missile armed bombers, all based in or near the United States. In this fashion cumulative American spending on NATO would be reduced over ten years from $2.2 trillion to only $900 billion. Ravenal concludes that while 'Finlandization' might be one outcome of this American reorientation, a more likely result would be a renewed emphasis in Europe on attending to their own security needs through regional cooperation and action.[36]

Ravenal and Towle together frame the defence-spending issue now facing Europe. Public opinion data, government pronouncements and national foreign policies all contribute to the debate. Ultimately, though, the complexities of international interdependence suggest that resolution of the European security issue will be determined by forces beyond the control of the actual states involved. Whether their response will be chaotic and *ad hoc* or reasoned and harmonized is ultimately what this study has sought to address.

NOTES

1. John Van Oudenaren, *U.S. Leadership Perceptions of the Soviet Problem Since 1945*, R-2843.NA (Santa Monica, CA: Rand, 1982).
2. Ibid., p. xi.
3. General Bernard Rogers, 'Follow-on Forces Attack (FOFA): Myths and Realities', *NATO Review*, 6 (December 1984), pp. 1–9.
4. Samuel F. Huntington, 'Conventional Deterrence and Conventional Retaliation in Europe', *International Security* (Winter 1983–4), p. 34.
5. William Tow, 'NATO's Out-of-Region Challenges to External Containment', *Orbis*, 28, 4 (Winter 1985), pp. 829–55.
6. France's participation in NATO is, naturally, limited only to political matters.
7. William Heiberg, *The Sixteenth Nation: Spain's Role in NATO*, series 83-1 (Washington, DC: NDU Press, 1983).
8. Panayote Dimitras, 'Greece: A New Danger', *Foreign Policy*, 58 (Spring 1985), pp. 134–50.
9. Trevor Taylor, *Defence Technology and International Integration* (New York: St Martin's Press, 1982), pp. 17–33.
10. Ibid., p. 24.

11. Ibid.
12. Decision Document of the First Ministerial IEPG, 22 and 23 November 1984, *NATO Review*, 6 (December 1984), pp. 28–9.
13. *NATO Today: The Alliance in Evolution*, a Report to the Committee on Foreign Relations, US Senate, April 1982, Chapter 5.
14. *Germany's Contribution to Western Defense* (New York: German Information Center, 1984), pp. 9–14.
15. *NATO: Agenda for the Next Four Years*, R-2836-FF (Santa Monica, CA: Rand, 1982), pp. 67–73.
16. Thomas A. Callaghan, Jr., 'The Structural Disarmament of NATO', *NATO Review*, June 1984, pp. 1–6.
17. Ibid., p. 1.
18. Ibid., p. 6.
19. *NATO Review*, 6 (December 1984), pp. 26–31.
20. Assembly of Western European Union, *Thirty Years of the Modified Brussels Treaty*, 30th ordinary session, 1st part, 15 May 1984, Doc. 973, p. 7.
21. Ibid. p. 8.
22. Assembly of Western European Union, *WEU, European Union and the Atlantic Alliance*, 30th ordinary session, Doc. 990, 30 October 1984.
23. European Parliament Working Document, *Report on Shared European Interests, Risks and Requirements in the Security Field*, 2 April 1984, Doc. 1-80/84/B, PE 88.462/B.
24. *New York Times*, 30 June 1985, p. 1.
25. Assembly of Western European Union, *WEU*, pp. 3–4.
26. Sixth Report from the Expenditure Committee, session 1978–9, H.C. 348, *The Future of the UK's Nuclear Weapons Policy*, House of Commons Defence and External Affairs Subcommittee (London: HMSO, 1979), p. 229.
27. Assembly of Western European Union, *Thirty Years of the Modified Brussels Treaty*, p. 19; personal interviews with NATO and American analysts, not for attribution.
28. Assembly of Western European Union, *WEU*, pp. 14–15.
29. 'Bid to Create a New European Dimension to Atlantic Pact', *The German Tribune*, 4 November 1984, p. 1.
30. David Greenwood, 'Strengthening Conventional Deterrence', *NATO Review*, August 1984, p. 11.
31. Assembly of Western European Union, *WEU*, p. 8.
32. Pierre Schwed and Henri Bagnouls, 'Vers une défense européenne', *Défense nationale* (October 1984), pp. 43–57.
33. Hedley Bull, 'European Self-reliance and the Reform of NATO', *Foreign Affairs*, 61, 4 (Spring 1983), p. 877.
34. Philip Towle, *Europe Without America: Can We Defend Ourselves?*, occasional paper no. 5 (London: Institute for European Defence and Strategic Studies, 1983).
35. Earl Ravenal 'Europe without America: The Erosion of NATO', *Foreign Affairs*, 63, 5 (1985), pp. 1020–35.
36. Ibid., pp. 1034–5.

7 Prospects

Studies on the Common Market habitually conclude with guidelines on what programmes, plans or policies should be implemented regionally to pursue a theoretic endpoint of political union. This study has suggested that the interplay of a complex interdependent manner of policy-making, which gains its coherence as a response to external actions, diminishes the primacy of internal programmes as a guide to regionally desirable initiatives. Given that orientation, prospects for a European security policy will depend on the nature of external challenges, in turn mandating a response even in the absence of regional agreement. Four such challenges corresponding to the intra-Alliance tensions discussed in Chapter 2 will then ultimately determine the shape, scope and potential of any European security policy.

Overarching in importance is the role of strategic weapons in a security policy grounded on a deterrent posture. To assert a coordinated European policy, in essence to reunite the damaged sovereignties of post-war Europe, yet remaining dependent on an ally for control over the fundamental assets of such a posture, is unacceptable. A further complication must be assumed with respect to the coupling of the American strategic arsenal to any defence of Europe. If a credible independent European strategic policy were to emerge, even as an adjunct of NATO, at some point a demand for greater Alliance responsibility will become visible. At the moment the dominant role of the United States is questioned so too must its willingness to risk destruction for Europe be rethought. If credibility is an issue in an Alliance system grounded on American dominance what would be the outcome of parity yet where only one partner had that ultimate strategic capability?

The immediate response might be to create a European strategic defence grounded on British and French nuclear assets. Aside from the immense political problems associated with this option, far greater costs would be incurred by the replacement of American assets with the far smaller, more vulnerable and less flexible European ones. It is one thing for British and French assets to be viewed as the ultimate guarantor of national sovereignty and quite another to assume the extended deterrence, flexible response stance now resting with the American arsenal.

When the issue is framed in this manner a continued reliance on the American deterrent and thus continued American primacy in the Alliance appears inevitable. Yet this study has sought to argue the divergence of American and European policies to a point where those guarantees may become incredible because of the fragmentation of the consensus basis on which they rest. In that case the need for a European security policy, rather than merely the desirability of one, becomes apparent. Perhaps, then, it is not too early to begin discussion on what shape it might have to assume; whether it must replicate identically American guarantees; or whether a new deterrent bargain more suitable to European foreign policy and defence objectives might instead be preferable.

The second challenge imposing itself on the articulation of a European security policy is political in nature, centering on the manner best suited to answering the American offer of a role in its SDI. The Canadian government, and more recently the West German government, stated that they would decline a direct government role in that project while still allowing its firms to take advantage of contracts and other opportunities associated with the project. That option, if pursued by Europe, would be self-defeating, signalling an inability to coordinate both the industrial and the foreign policy components of a regional security policy. Fragmentation redounding to the short-term benefit of the United States government and selected MNEs would mandate long-term negative consequences for Europe. Only by coordination through the suggested ETP can these negative effects be overcome and policy coherence and direction be assured. Therefore the European response to the SDI offer may be the single best measure of the level of foreign policy cohesion existing within the Common Market when it is faced with a variety of decision options whose long-term effects are, for the most part, already known.

The third concern revolves about a possible American initiated trade war with severe implications for a European security policy. Although President Reagan has threatened to impose sanctions on selected European goods and commodities, as yet these measures have not reached the dual use sector with its direct security implications. To gain the ability to compete against the United States in these dual use items one must also acknowledge the protectionist tendencies that will arise in support of domestic industries. What is being termed in some American academic circles 'new wave economics' expressly supports the imposition of import controls in these new technological sectors.

To counter this American action requires a Europe coordinating its response so as to create a parity relationship between the two regions capable of negotiating offsets to potential protectionist measures. A fragmented Europe would have little chance of assuming that role. The recent personal appeal of Prime Minister Thatcher to President Reagan in support of the American purchase of a British rather than a French military system, because of her support of the SDI, is absolutely inimical to the development of this coordinated European policy. Only through the instrument of the ETP can such independent national stances be submerged within a regionally directed policy response.

Finally, the role of public opinion remains to be queried on its potential role in the development of a European security policy. Perhaps the best indicator in this area would be the outcome of elections or realignments now anticipated in Britain, West Germany and France. The possibility of the Labour Party and the SPD returning to power in the first two states and the distinct chance of a conservative Assembly and a socialist President in France strongly suggest the diminution of any ability to define a coherent European security policy after those realignments. Although elections are a response to nationally defined issues they can also redound to the detriment of regionally desirable policies. Adoption of the ETP would allow security issues to be insulated from the effects of national elections thereby increasing the coherence and longevity of regional initiatives. Of course, care must be taken to ensure that European policies remain receptive to democratic values rather than becoming a function of centrally directed bureaucracies. A mixture is essential to ensure responsiveness yet within the ambit of regional objectives. Ultimately any European security policy must rest on a blend of citizen, member and regional inputs. That mixture, then, is Europe's strength and unfortunately also its weakness. For that reason the outcome of a European security policy, no matter how necessary, remains at this point more a matter of hope than certainty.

Index

ABMS *see* ballistic missiles
aerospace industry 51, 57–62, 78, 89–91
  Airbus project xxv, 8, 50, 60, 62, 78, 99–100, 107
  Arianespace 95–6
  B-1 bomber 15, 117–18
  EFA 78, 89–91, 99–100, 105, 122
  Harrier aircraft 114, 122
  helicopters 114
  Mirage project 57, 105
  Tornado project xxv, 50, 57, 59, 68, 90, 99–100, 120, 122
Afghanistan 14, 72
Agfa-Gevaert 48
agriculture xvii, 7, 73, 81
  CAP xvi, xxi, 81
Airbus project xxv, 8, 50, 60, 62, 78, 99–100, 101
America *see* USA
anti-ballistic missiles *see* ballistic missiles
anti-submarine warfare *see* ASW
Arianespace 95–6
armaments *see* defence procurement
ASW 121
asymmetric dependence *see* complex interdependence
AT & T 88

B-1 bomber 15, 118
ballistic missiles 13, 15
BAOR 121
Belgium *see* Benelux countries
Benelux countries 5, 18 *see also* EC
Boeing 100, 120
Bretton Woods agreement 3
British Airways 58
British Army of the Rhine *see* BAOR
business mergers 48–9

Canada xix
CAP xvi, xxi, 81
Caterpillar 73
Carter administration 8, 14, 20
CAVE workshops 88

CDCs 51, 56, 83–4
Chrysler 49
COBOL language 55
COCOM Committee 25, 76–7
Columbus project 96, 97
Common Agricultural Policy *see* CAP
communications xxv–xxvi
Community Development Contracts *see* CDCs
Community Premium Scheme 56
Community Social Fund 51
complex interdependence xxiv–xxvii, 7
computer industry *see* data processing industry
containment 2, 19–22
Coordinating Committee Consultative Group *see* COCOM
COPERS 95
cruise missiles 15, 37, 40
Cuba 8
Czechoslovakia 3

data processing industry 5, 11, 54–7, 85–9
  see also informatics industry; IT
defence *see* security
defence procurement 70–1, 89–91, 114, 122, 124–5
defence spin-offs 64–72, 76, 91–2, 93
Denmark 102, 105
  and NATO 121
Department of Commerce (USA) 76–7
Department of Defense (USA) *see* DOD
détente 13, 19–22
deterrance 10–19
development *see* research and development
DOD 16–17, 30, 65, 76–7, 94
Dooge Committee 102, 123

EADA 69
EAPA 69, 91, 125
EC
  aerospace industry 57–62
  and Third World countries 25
  and USA 2–9, 11–19, 20–6, 34–6, 45–63, 73–9, 85–7, 109–12
  and USSR 19–22, 34, 36

EC (*cont.*)
  CAP xvi, xxi, 81
  communications xxv, xxvi
  data processing industry 54–7
  economic relations 22–6, 70–1
  Esprit project 84, 87–9, 97, 101, 105
  ETP 101–6, 120, 125, 129, 130
  Eureka project xxv, xxvi, 94, 97, 103
  export controls 72–9
  high technology industries 45–63
  Industrial Policy xxv, 52–62
  informatics industry 52–64
  integration xv–xxiii, 48–9, 50–62, 69
  interdependence xxiv–xxvii
  nuclear weapons in 10, 11–12
  political objectives xv
  Premium Scheme 56
  security 2–3, 4, 5, 6, 10–19, 20–2
  security policy xxi–xxiv, xxvi, 21–2, 27, 33–42, 97–101, 81–108, 109–27
  security relationships xv, xxi–xxiii, 4–5, 10–44, 111–13, 122–4
  Social Fund 51
  technology transfers 72
  'two-speed' xv–xvi, xxiii, 102
  USA troops in 1–2, 11, 114
  see also EEC; individual countries; NATO
economic aid
  Marshall Plan 3, 11, 22, 29
economic relations 22–6
economic resources 6–7, 8–9
  and security xv, 26–33, 64–72, 114–18, 125–6
  new wave 129
  see also oil supplies; socio-economics
ECSC xvii, 5, 82, 118–19
ECU 82, 85, 86, 87
EDC 4, 38, 84–5, 99, 110, 119
EEB 51, 83, 84–5, 99
EEC 5, 7, 74–5
  see also EC; individual countries
EFA 78, 89–91, 99–100, 105, 122
EIB 83
EIL 84–5
Eisenhower administration 2–3, 11–12
ELDO 95
Electric Boat Co. 98
electronics industry 56, 57, 86
embargoes 25–6
  see also export controls; protectionism
emerging technologies *see* ETs
EMS 9, 24–5, 81, 84, 98
EMU 82, 84
EPC 22, 105, 123
ESA 95–7, 125
Esprit project 84, 87–9, 97, 101, 105
  see also informatics industry; IT

ESRO 95
ETs 19
  see also high-technology industries; IT
ETP 101–6, 120, 125, 129, 130
Euratom xvii, 5
Eureka project xxv, xxvi, 94, 97, 103
Eurogroup 114, 119
Europe *see* EC
European Armament Procurement Agency *see* EAPA
European Coal and Steel Community *see* ECSC
European Community *see* EC
European Company *see* SE
European Council xix, 55, 69, 83, 87
European Defence Analysis Bureau *see* EADA
European Defence Community *see* EDC
European Development Contracts *see* CDCs
European Economic Community *see* EEC
European Export Bank *see* EEB
European Fighter Aircraft *see* EFA
European Financial Agency 85
European Innovation Loan *see* EIL
European integration xv–xxiii, 48–9, 50–62, 69
European Investment Bank *see* EIB
European Launcher Development Organization *see* ELDO
European Monetary System *see* EMS
European Monetary Union *see* EMU
European Parliament xix, xxvi, 55, 69, 83
European Political Cooperation *see* EPC
European Space Agency *see* ESA
European Space Research Organization *see* ESRO
European Strategic Programme for Research and Development in Innovation technologies *see* Esprit project
European Technology Policy *see* ETP
exchange rates *see* foreign exchange
EXIM 82–3
export controls 72–9
  see also embargoes; protectionism
Export-Import Bank *see* EXIM
exports 72, 82–5
extraterritoriality 72, 73

Falklands war 112
federalism xix–xx
Fergusson Report 70, 71
financing *see* investment
FOFA 111
foreign aid *see* economic aid; military aid
foreign exchange 6–7, 9, 24, 32, 49
foreign policy
  public attitudes to 34–42
  USA 1–9, 11–19, 20–2

USSR 1–3, 5, 6, 8, 11–22
  see also security
foreign relations *see* international relations
foreign trade *see* international trade
France 3, 5, 15, 128–30
  and NATO 4, 111
  high-technology industries 48, 54
  Plan Calcul 54
  security 29, 31, 92–3, 94
  space research 95–6
  see also EC
functionalism xvii–xviii

GATT 3, 105
  Dillon Round 3
  Tokyo Round 8, 78–9, 101
Gazelle helicopter 114
General Agreement on Tariffs and Trade *see* GATT
Genscher-Colombo proposal 123
Germany *see* West Germany
Great Britain *see* UK
Greece xxvii, 2, 81, 95, 102, 105
  and NATO 112–13, 121
  see also EC
Greenwood Report 69, 70
Grenada 14

Harrier aircraft 114, 122
helicopters 114
Hermes shuttle 96
high-technology industries 23, 31, 45–63, 64, 72–9, 81–9
  see also ETs; IT; technology gap
Honeywell 52
Hot missiles 114
Hungary 3, 12

IBM 47, 52–4, 55, 88, 98, 100
ICL 52, 53, 55
IEPG 114, 117, 119, 123
Industrial Policy xxv, 52–62, 69
Industrial Reorganization Corporation *see* IRC
industry
  aerospace 51, 57–62, 78, 89–91
  cooperation in xvii, xxi
  defence procurement 70–1, 89–91, 114, 122, 124–5
  defence spin-offs 64–72, 76, 91–2, 93
  ETs 19
  high-technology 23, 31, 45–63, 64, 72–9, 81–9
  MNEs 3–4, 7, 23, 45–63, 64–5, 73, 84, 86, 97–101
  service xvii, 24, 31

steel 104
textile 51, 104
informatics industry 52–7
  Esprit project 84, 87–9, 97, 101, 105
  see also data processing industry; IT
innovations technology *see* IT
Institute for Industrial Reconstruction *see* IRI
integration xxi–xxiii
  definition xvi
  European xv–xxiii, 48–9, 50–62, 69
  security xvii–xviii
  theories of xvi–xxi
  vertical 47
  see also interdependence
interdependence xxi–xxiii
  and EC xxiv–xxvii
  and security policy xxiii–xxiv
  complex xxiv–xxvii
  theory xxii–xxiv
  see also integration
intermediate-range nuclear force *see* INF
International Business Machines *see* IBM
International Computers Ltd *see* ICL
international law 72–5, 99
international relations xxvi–xxviii, 1–9
  in Europe 10–44
  Ostpolitik 13, 20, 25
  see also individual countries
international trade xxi, 7, 22–6, 46–54, 57–60, 64
  defence procurement 70–1, 89–91, 114, 122, 124–5
  trade wars 22–6, 129–30
  investment 48–62, 64–72, 81–9
  primary aid 66
  secondary aid 65–6
IRC 48
Ireland 105
IRI 48
IT 85–9
  Esprit project 84, 87–9, 97, 101, 105
  see also data processing industry; informatics industry
isolationism 1, 2, 11
Italy xvii, 5, 18
  and NATO 112, 113
  high-technology industries 48
  see also EC

Japan 24, 49, 64, 85–6
Johnson administration 27

Kennedy administration 5–6, 12, 27
Kissinger Proposals 20–1
Klepsch Report 69, 70, 89, 91, 125
Korean war 2, 11–12

Lebanon 14, 21
linkage 13, 19
Lisbon Conference 1952 2
Lomé Convention 24
London Conference 1954 119
London Conference 1981 123
Lynx helicopter 114

Marshall Plan 3, 11, 22, 29
Middle East 70, 111
  see also OPEC
Milan missiles 14
Milan Summit 1985 102–3, 121
military aid 2–3, 5–6
military strategy 111–12, 120–1
  see also security
Mirage project 57, 105
missiles
  ABMS 13
  ballistic 13, 15, 91
  cruise 15, 37, 40
  Hot 114
  Milan 114
  MX 15
  Pershing IIs 18, 40, 92
  SS-20s 18, 92
  see also nuclear weapons; SDI
MLF 38, 110
MNEs
  American 3–4, 7, 23, 45–63, 64–5, 73, 84, 86
  European 97–101
MRCA *see* Tornado project
multilateral force *see* MLF
multi-national enterprises *see* MNEs
Multi-Role Combat Aircraft *see* Tornado project
MX missiles 15

NASA 27, 49, 53, 58
  and European projects 94, 95, 96
National Aeronautics and Space Administration *see* NASA
NATO xv, 11, 76, 105
  and USA xxiv, 2, 4, 12–13, 14–15, 18–19, 20, 109–27
  attitudes to 34, 36–42
  funding 32, 114–18
  future of 36–8, 128–9
  Nunn amendment 15, 20, 114
  relationships in xxiv, xxvii, 4, 113–18, 122–4
  supplies for 71, 90, 100, 124–5
  treaty 4, 119
  'twin-track' policy 10–11, 14, 18, 36–7, 40
  'two-way' street 69, 71, 90, 113–14, 124–5
  see also EC; security
neo-functionalism xx–xxi

Netherlands xix, 18 *see also* EC
neutralism 34–40, 105
  see also pacificism; protest movement
New Look 2–3, 5, 11–12
new wave economics 129
Nicaragua 72
Nixon administration 6, 13, 20
North Atlantic Treaty Organization *see* NATO
nuclear weapons 2–3, 6
  in Europe 10, 11–12
  see also missiles; SDI
Nunn Amendment 15, 20, 114

oil supplies 25, 31, 39, 73–4, 112
OPEC xxii, xxiv–xxv, 7, 49
  see also Middle East
Organization of Petroleum Exporting Countries *see* OPEC
Ostpolitik 13, 20, 25

pacificism 33, 39–40, 109
  see also neutralism; protest movements
Paris Summit 1972 xix, 83, 102
peace movements *see* protest movements
Pershing II missiles 18, 40, 92
Plan Calcul 54
pluralism xviii
Poland 72
policy integration xxii
political community xxii
political objectives xv, xvii, xxi–xxii, 71–2
Portugal 95
  and NATO 113
Premium Scheme *see* Community Premium Scheme
Preparatory Commission for European Space Research *see* COPERS
primary aid 66–7
  see also investment
protectionism 8, 23, 25–6, 48–9, 67, 114
  see also embargoes; export controls
protest movements 18, 39, 40–2
  see also neutralism; pacificism
public opinion 33–42
Puma helicopter 14

RA Index xviii
Reagan administration 8, 14, 15, 25, 26, 27, 28–9, 74–5, 77, 93, 113, 129, 130
regional integration *see* integration
Relative Acceptance Index *see* RA Index
research and development 48, 50, 51, 65–6, 68, 70
  see also IT
Roland missiles 114
Rome Conference 1984 123

Rome Treaty 22–3, 82–3, 98–9
Russia *see* USSR

SAC 120, 124–5
SALT 10, 13
SDI xxvi, 15, 26, 75, 89, 92–4, 99, 102, 103, 111,
    129–30
SE 83
secondary aid 65–7
    see also investment
security
    and economic resources xv, 26–33, 64–72,
        114–18, 125–6
    attitudes to 34–42
    deterrance 10–19
    European 2–3, 4, 5, 6, 10–44, 81–108, 97–
        101, 109–27, 128–30
    integration xvii–xviii
    interdependence xxiii–xxvii
    military strategy 111–12, 120–2
    policy xxi–xxiv, xxvi, 21–2, 27, 33–42, 81–
        108, 97–101, 109–27, 128–30
    relationships xv, xxi–xxiii, 21–2
    SDI xxvi, 15, 26, 75, 89, 92–4, 99, 102, 103,
        111, 129–30
    tensions 10–44
    USA 2, 5–6, 11–19
    see also NATO
sensitivity xxiii–xxiv
service industries xvii, 24, 31
Siemens 88
socio-economics xvii, xx, 26–33, 51
    see also economic resources
sovereignty 1–9
Soviet Union *see* USSR
space programmes 91–7
    Columbus 96, 97
    Eureka 94, 97, 103
    European 94–7
    Hermes 96
    SDI xxvi, 15, 26, 75, 89, 92–4, 99, 102, 103,
        111, 129–30
    shuttle 91, 96
    Spacelab 95
Spain xxvii
    and NATO 112–13
    see also EC
SS-20 missiles 18, 92
Standard Telecom Laboratories 88
Standing Armaments Committee *see* SAC
steel industry 104
Strategic Arms Limitation Talks *see* SALT
Strategic Defence Initiative *see* SDI
submarines
    ASW 121
    Trident 71, 98, 114, 121
symmetrical response 20

taxation 73
technical cooperation *see* industrial coopera-
    tion
technology gap 64, 65
technology transfers 72
telecommunications industry 56
textile industry 51, 104
Thatcher administration 93, 102–3, 130
Third World countries 25, 51, 67, 68, 85, 112
    arms sales to 71
    space requirements 96
Tornado project xxv, 50, 57, 59, 68, 90, 99–
    100, 120, 122
trade wars 22–6, 129–30
Treaty of Rome *see* Rome Treaty
Trident programme 71, 98, 114, 121
Truman Doctrine 2, 11
Turkey
    and NATO 112–13
'twin-track' policy 10–11, 14, 18, 36–7, 40
'two-speed' Community xv–xvi, xxiii, 102
'two-way' street policy 69, 71, 90, 113–14,
    124–5

UK 3, 7, 23, 33, 81, 102–3, 113, 128–30
    and NATO 15, 18, 112, 121–2
    and USA 121–2
    and WEU 123–4
    high-technology industries 48, 53
    security 29, 31, 93
    Thatcher administration 93, 102–3, 130
    see also EC
Unidata 50, 52, 53, 88
unification *see* integration
United Kingdom *see* UK
United States of America *see* USA
UNIX system 88
USA 64
    and EC 2–9, 11–19, 20–6, 34–6, 54–63, 73–
        9, 85–7, 109–12
    and NATO xxiv, 2, 4, 12–13, 14–15, 18–19,
        20, 109–27
    and UK 121–2
    and USSR 1–3, 5, 6, 8, 11–19, 25, 92–4,
        109–12
    Carter administration 8, 14, 20
    Eisenhower administration 2–3, 11–12
    foreign relations 1–9
    high-technology industries 45–63
    Johnson administration 27
    Kennedy administration 5–6, 12, 27
    Marshall Plan 3, 11, 22, 29
    MNEs 3–4, 7, 23, 45–63, 64–5, 73, 84, 86
    New Look 2–3, 5, 11–12
    Nixon administration 6, 13, 20
    Reagan administration 8, 14, 15, 25, 26, 27,
        28–9, 74–5, 77, 93, 113, 129, 130

USA (*cont.*)
  SDI xxvi, 15, 26, 75, 89, 92–4, 99, 102, 103, 111, 120–30
  security funding 2, 5–6, 11–29
  Southern Command 27
  troops in Europe 1–2, 11, 114
  Truman doctrine 2, 11

USSR
  and Afghanistan 14
  and EC 19–22, 34, 36
  and USA 1–3, 5, 6, 8, 11–19, 25, 92–4, 109–12
  and West Germany 25

vertical integration 47

Vietnam war 5–6, 12–13, 58
vulnerability xiii–xxiv

welfare programmes *see* socio-economics
West Germany xxvii, 3, 5, 13–14, 19, 77, 81, 128–30
  and NATO 4, 18, 121
  and USSR 25
  arms sales 70
  security 92–3, 94, 110, 111
Western European Union *see* WEU
Western Union Defence Organization *see* WUDO
WEU xxv, 4, 71, 94, 101–2, 105, 118–19, 121, 122–4
  SAC 120, 124–5
WUDO 119